YOU'VE LOST IT, NOW WHAT?

YOU'VE LOST IT, NOW WHAT?

HOW TO BEAT
THE BEAR MARKET
AND STILL RETIRE ON TIME

Jonathan Clements

Portfolio

Portfolio
Published by the Penguin Group
Penguin Group (USA) Inc., 375 Hudson Street,
New York, New York 10014, U.S.A.
Penguin Books Ltd, 80 Strand,
London WC2R 0RL, England
Penguin Books Australia Ltd, 250 Camberwell Road, Camberwell,
Victoria 3124, Australia
Penguin Books Canada Ltd, 10 Alcorn Avenue,
Toronto, Ontario, Canada M4V 3B2
Penguin Books India (P) Ltd, 11 Community Centre, Panchsheel Park,
New Delhi—110 017, India
Penguin Books (N.Z.) Ltd, Cnr Rosedale and Airborne Roads, Albany,
Auckland, New Zealand
Penguin Books (South Africa) (Pty) Ltd, 24 Sturdee Avenue,
Rosebank, Johannesburg 2196, South Africa

Penguin Books Ltd, Registered Offices:
Harmondsworth, Middlesex, England

First published in 2003 by Viking Penguin,
a member of Penguin Group (USA) Inc.

1 3 5 7 9 10 8 6 4 2

This publication is designed to provide accurate and authoritative information in regard to the subject matter covered. It is sold with the understanding that the publisher is not engaged in rendering legal, accounting or other professional services. If you require legal advice or other expert assistance, you should seek the services of a competent individual.

Library of Congress Cataloging-in-Publication Data
Clements, Jonathan.
    You've lost it, now what? : how to beat the bear market and still retire on time /
Jonathan Clements.
       p. cm.
    Includes index.
    "Web sites" : P . .
    ISBN 1-59184-016-3
       1. Finance, Personal.   2. Retirement income—Planning.   3. Investments.
    4. Stocks.   I. Title: How to beat the bear market and still retire on time.
    II. Title.
    HG179.C6513 2003
    332.024'01—dc21   2003040495

This book is printed on acid-free paper. ∞

Printed in the United States of America

For my mother and father

ACKNOWLEDGMENTS

Most books start with a bright idea from the author. This book started with a phone call from Penguin Putnam editor Adrian Zackheim. What, he wondered, should investors do now? If your portolio has been devastated by the stock-market collapse, how do you make sure you can retire on time? If you are already retired, how can you bounce back from the massive financial hit of the past three years? Adrian wanted a book that would answer these critical questions.

I jumped at the chance. For years, through my weekly columns for *The Wall Street Journal* and *The Wall Street Journal Sunday*, I have tried to help readers understand the bewildering world of Wall Street. More recently, writing those columns has seemed like 24-hour triage, as I struggled to keep investors on track through the brutal stock-market decline. Here, thanks to Adrian, was a chance to take a step back and offer readers a roadmap for the journey ahead.

Writing a book is one of the great selfish acts. The author gets all the credit. Those unlucky enough to be nearby both help and suffer, and yet they receive only the briefest of mentions. On that score, my first brief mention goes to my agent, Wesley Neff. I often tell friends that Wes has the literary sensibilities of an English major and the negotiating tactics of a Mafia don. It's a joke, of course. Well, sort of.

To critique the manuscript, I turned to three of the investment experts I admire most: William Bernstein, David Foster, and Chris Mayer. My thanks. I also couldn't have written this book without the help of *The Wall Street Journal* editors David Crook, Edward Felsenthal, Daniel Hertzberg, and Neal Templin. All cut me a little slack at work, thus freeing up time to write this book. (True, Neal, you didn't cut me that much slack. But I am trying to be kind. OK?)

As with my earlier books, Hannah and Henry knew when to stay out of the way. "Dad's working on his book again," came the murmur from the other room. I was never sure whether it was said with sympathy or rolled eyes. But my heart grew fonder with their absences.

My partner, Carolyn, suffered this book more than anyone. In our crazy world of frantic schedules and petulant cats, her kindness and smiles kept me sane. "I am wiped out," I would announce at the end of another long day. "I am shocked," Carolyn would reply. But she never was.

Finally, this book is dedicated to my mother and father. After all that you have given me, it is not much to give in return. You have been great parents. But you have been even greater friends.

CONTENTS

YOU'VE LOST IT, NOW WHAT?

1 LOSING IT

There is hope.

Almost every day, I hear another tale of financial woe, the family that banked everything on Internet stocks, the WorldCom employee whose 401(k) was wiped out by the stock's collapse, the shell-shocked couple who retired early, only to see their nest egg sliced in half. There is, without a doubt, a lot of financial pain.

But there is also hope. Even if you have lost 40 percent, 50 percent, or even 80 percent of your savings, it is still possible to retire in comfort. This book will help you do just that. In the pages ahead, I will detail the lessons of the stock-market crash and help you sort through today's barrage of dubious advice and unremitting angst. I will tell how best to invest in stocks, bonds, and real estate and I'll talk about the likely return from owning each. I will discuss how to rebuild your nest egg and, once you quit the work force, how to squeeze maximum income out of your retirement savings.

But in the end, you will have to save yourself. Don't expect to get bailed out by another dazzling bull market. In the decade ahead, returns are likely to be modest and certainly far below the 18.2 percent a year clocked by the Standard & Poor's 500-stock index in the 1990s. Instead, to amass enough for retirement, you will need to settle on a prudent investment plan, move decisively to straighten out your portfolio, keep your worst instincts at bay, and save like crazy. Sound daunting? If anything, it should be liberating. For the past three years, your portfolio has been kicked around by a crazy market. Now, it is time to reclaim control of your financial life.

No, you can't control the market's direction. But there is much that you can control, including how much risk you take, how much you incur in investment costs and taxes, how much you save and spend, and how you react to the market's ups and downs. At first blush, these may not seem like the key drivers of your portfolio's performance. But if you get these items under control, better investment results will almost certainly follow.

INVESTORS BEHAVING BADLY

Irrational exuberance. Ah, those were the good old days.

Of course, it didn't start exuberantly. The great bull market of the 1990s started rather tamely, with the economy growing year after year, productivity climbing at a surprising clip, and inflation remaining remarkably subdued. The world was at peace and times were undoubtedly good.

Stocks had been rising fairly steadily since 1982, with only brief setbacks in 1984, 1987, and 1990. Why shouldn't the good times keep on rolling? By the mid-1990s, investors had grown comfortable with the market. Money started gushing into stocks and stock funds and the market's rise began to quicken. After a lackluster 1994, the S&P 500 leapt 37 percent in 1995 and then jumped another 23 percent in 1996, according to Ibbotson Associates, a Chicago research firm that provided much of the historical market data used in this book.

Investors had caught the scent of easy money. Initially, however, their passion tended toward the prosaic. As many folks made their first foray into the market, they favored the big blue-chip stocks they knew and loved. Money flooded into large-company stock funds, especially index funds that track the performance of the S&P 500. For their scant courage, buyers were handsomely rewarded, with the S&P 500 climbing 33 percent in 1997, 29 percent in 1998, and 21 percent in 1999. These numbers are total returns, which means that they reflect both share-price gains and reinvested dividends.

But while dull proved comfortably rewarding, even bigger profits were there to be had. The easy money minted in blue chips was quickly eclipsed by evenheadier performance from technology shares, particularly Internet stocks. It all came in a maddening rush, huge stock-market gains instantly rewarding technological innovations. One moment, people were buying their first computer and tentatively venturing onto the World Wide Web. The next moment, they were gathered in chat rooms, trying to figure out how to make a few bucks off this puppy.

Computers were selling like hot cakes, Internet usage was exploding, and the possibilities seemed limitless, with everything from pet supplies to pornography available with just a few quick strokes of the keyboard. The New Economy. The New Paradigm. The New Era. No more recessions. No more inflation. Making money in stocks was a breeze. In fact, making money wasn't the problem. The problem was, everybody else seemed to be making so much more. In the late 1990s, the S&P 500 scored over 20 percent every year for five consecutive years, and yet that seemed like pocket change compared to the huge winnings offered by tech stocks.

We were supposed to be having fun. But it didn't seem like fun. One wag quipped, "Never has a bull market been enjoyed so little by so many." We knew TheGlobe.com, Global Crossing, and JDS Uniphase were headed higher. We just didn't know why. We knew stocks were ridiculously expensive. Yet they kept on rising. It was a bewildering blizzard of B2Bs, VCs, and CNBC. Investors spent their evenings trolling for stock tips on Internet bulletin boards and their days feverishly trading on the fruits of their research.

Happiness was 100 shares of an initial public stock offering. But which IPO? It didn't seem to matter. As long as the business plan mentioned the Internet, a $1 billion stock-market capitalization was all but assured. What about sales? Unnecessary. Profits? Don't even ask. We talked eyeballs and burn rates and pretended that it all made sense.

Even mutual funds boasted of 100 percent-plus annual gains. But in the bull market, funds seemed like stocks with training wheels. What you really needed were individual technology stocks, preferably Internet stocks, and, better still, Internet stocks bought by borrowing on margin.

In 1999, James Glassman and Kevin Hassett came out with their now-infamous book, *Dow 36,000*, which argued that stocks were no riskier than bonds and thus the Dow Jones Industrial Average deserved to be at more than triple its current level. Foolish books are published all the time, so that wasn't a big surprise. And foolish books often become best-sellers, so that wasn't a big surprise, either. No, the big surprise was this: People took *Dow 36,000* seriously.

I found myself plodding along, writing my weekly column for *The Wall Street Journal*. I had been a long-time advocate of stock-market investing, so I wasn't about to dissuade readers from investing in stocks. But I also warned investors to temper their expectations and persistently preached the virtues of spreading your investment bets widely. Colleagues considered me a bull. Readers deemed me a wimp.

"You just don't get it," screamed my e-mail correspondents. I remember one message in particular. It arrived just as the market was peaking and followed yet another of my dull discourses on diversification. "The technology sector is so big and so diverse," wrote my correspondent, "that you don't need to own any other stocks. All you need to do is buy different types of technology companies and you will be well diversified."

Stocks peaked in March 2000. But for me, the market top didn't come until the summer. That was when my two kids returned from a trip to New Hampshire, where they had visited their cousins. "Uncle Dave's a millionaire, Uncle Dave's a millionaire," Henry and Hannah chanted as they danced around the living room. Uncle Dave was a top-notch computer programmer at a start-up company that had just gone public. The details poured out in a verbal flood: early retirement, a bigger house, Aunt Lydia worrying about how the money would change them all.

In the heady days immediately after the IPO, the stock briefly traded above $150. But almost immediately, Uncle Dave's newly found wealth began to ebb away.

Like a commentator at a prizefight, my daughter would keep me apprised of the company's fortunes. "The stock's fallen below $100," Hannah would announce, her voice gripped with drama. "It's down to $80," came the next breathless dispatch. By the end of 2000, the shares were at less than $25 and my market commentator had fallen silent. Finally, two years later, I asked for an update. "It's under $2," Hannah offered with a shrug.

LOSING YOUR SHIRT

It hasn't been pleasant. But it does rank as one of history's great stock-market collapses. Initially, share prices were hammered lower by renewed inflation and a sharp rise in short-term interest rates orchestrated by the Federal Reserve. By the fall of 2000, investors were fretting about higher oil prices and a disputed presidential election.

The following year brought recession, California's energy crisis, dismal earnings growth, the September 11 terrorist attacks, and war in Afghanistan. By late 2001 and 2002, concern had turned to a slew of accounting scandals, worries that the economy could slip back into recession, and fear of what a war with Iraq might mean. The decline, it seemed, was unstoppable. Every time the market appeared to hit bottom, more bad news came along to drive share prices lower.

How bad has it been? In the 1929–32 crash, the Dow Jones Industrial Average plunged 89 percent over 34 months. In the 1973–74 crash, the Dow industrials shed 45 percent and the decline took 23 months. These figures exclude dividends, which would reduce the losses somewhat.

Today's market may have more carnage to offer and the lows we saw in late 2002 may not mark the end of the bear market. But already, there has been plenty of financial pain, with the stock market losing $8.5 trillion of value over the 31 months through October 2002, according to Wilshire Associates. That $8.5 trillion loss wasn't suffered just by small investors. Pension plans, endowments, and foreign investors are all big holders of U.S. stocks. Still, many mom-and-pop investors have seen their portfolios trashed. According to the Investment Company Institute and the Securities Industry Association, almost half of all households owned stocks or stock funds as of early 2002.

The kindest view of the decline comes from looking at the Dow Jones Industrial Average, which fell 38 percent from its January 14, 2000, peak to its low on October 9, 2002. Now, a 38 percent plunge may seem pretty severe. But the Dow's loss has been small potatoes compared to the blow suffered by the S&P 500 and the Nasdaq Composite Index.

Think of the S&P 500 as representative of the broad market. From its March 24, 2000, peak to the market trough on October 9, 2002, the S&P 500 lost 49 percent. That was the sort of loss endured by the typical stock investor. Meanwhile, consider the Nasdaq Composite Index to be a gauge of technology stocks. It lost a staggering 78 percent from March 10, 2000, to its 2002 low, which also occurred October 9. That was the sort of hit you took if you had banked heavily on technology stocks.

Few people would actually be sitting with a stock

portfolio that is 78 percent underwater. I doubt that many investors committed their entire portfolio to stocks in March 2000 and sold everything in October 2002. Most would have put money into stocks ahead of the market peak, so they enjoyed some of the run-up, and these folks would have either bailed out of stocks before they reached bottom or held on, waiting for a rebound before selling.

Nonetheless, let us assume that you were dunned for the full loss suffered by the Nasdaq. What will it take to get back to even? Unfortunately, the math of investment losses is brutal. If your portfolio had been worth $100,000 at the market peak, a 78 percent thrashing would leave you with just $22,000. If you then enjoyed a 78 percent rebound, that would only get you back to $39,160. Instead, to recover your full $78,000 loss and get back to $100,000, you will need a 355 percent gain. At 7 percent a year, it would take a grueling 22 years to earn that much.

You are in better shape if your losses mirror the broad market. Once again, assume that your portfolio was worth $100,000 at the height of the bull market. After a 49 percent loss, you would be down to $51,000. To recoup your $49,000 loss and get back to $100,000, you will need a 96 percent gain. It will take a little under 10 years to make that sort of money, assuming that you earn 7 percent a year.

To be sure, the losses suffered have been horrifying and the road ahead seems arduous. But if you save diligently and invest intelligently, you should be able to cut your portfolio's recovery time and quickly get yourself back on track for retirement. This is not the moment for panicky decisions. Yet many people, I fear, long ago abandoned all pretense of long-term investing.

LOSING YOUR COMPOSURE

As the bear market dragged on through 2001 and 2002 and investors' losses mounted, the whirl of emotions became more vicious. Rudyard Kipling may have advised readers, "Keep your head when all about you are losing theirs." But Mr. Kipling clearly never owned an Internet stock that lost 90 percent of its value. It is awfully tough to stay calm when your wealth seems to shrink every time the stock market opens for business.

According to Wall Street lore, when stocks plunge, investors panic and sell. But the reality is a little more complicated than that. Even if you are not dumping every share you own, you may not be behaving in an entirely rational manner.

How do you stop yourself from making decisions you will likely later regret? Take a deep breath and ponder some of the thoughts racing through your mind. Thinking clearly? Maybe not. The odds are, you have entertained at least some of the notions listed below.

"When I get even, I'll get out." Experts in investor psychology say that the pain we get from losses is more than twice as great as the pleasure we get from gains.

Suppose your sister offers you the chance to bet on a coin flip, where losing would cost you $100. To entice you to bet, how much would winning have to be worth? Given that the chance of guessing heads or tails correctly is 50 percent, a $100 prize should be sufficient. But in all likelihood, to get you to play, your sister would have to offer the opportunity to win over $200.

The implication: Winning may be fun, but losing really stings. It is not simply that this great bear market has left us poorer. We also feel pretty darn stupid. What in the world were we thinking when we put so much money into stocks? This sense of regret stops us from selling. After all, if we bail out now, not only do we give up all chance of making back our losses, but also we will be forced to admit that we made a colossal blunder.

This refusal to sell at a loss isn't such a bad instinct. In fact, it could be your financial salvation. If you own a sensible, well-diversified portfolio, your reluctance to sell may keep you invested, so that you benefit from the eventual market rebound.

As the market recovers, however, you will need to remain vigilant. With any luck, rising share prices will calm your frayed nerves and you will choose to stick with stocks for the long haul. But what if you are determined to get out as soon as you get back to even? Be careful not to jump the gun.

As the market malaise drags on, you may be tempted to lower what you consider your "break-even" price. Forget making back your full loss. Maybe you will be happy if the Dow Jones Industrial Average gets back to 11,000, or 10,000, or wherever it was last time you dared look at your account statements. There is a risk that you will sell too soon, suffering the full brunt of the bear market, but getting little benefit from the subsequent recovery.

"Stocks always bounce back." Truth be told, if you currently hold a prudent portfolio, I am not too worried. If you had a sensible portfolio to begin with, you will probably continue to behave sensibly.

What if you have a lopsided portfolio that is heavily invested in a few stocks or a single sector? Now, I am worried. The problem isn't that you might sell too soon. Rather, the problem is you may never sell. You made the mistake of buying a bonehead portfolio. But now, you may compound that error by refusing to sell at a loss. My fear: The "get even, then get out" syndrome will cause you to sit tight, instead of fixing a portfolio that desperately needs to be repaired.

Just because a stock is down 70 or 80 percent doesn't mean that it won't fall further. Even from today's depressed levels, technology stocks could continue to sink. Think about the decline of the Nasdaq Composite Index over the past few years. From March to December 2000, the Nasdaq index was cut in half, as tech stocks were hammered lower. But even after that great hit, it would have been smart to sell. After all, from that depressed level, the index was cut in half again, so that investors soon had just a quarter of what they started with.

Moreover, depending on what sort of portfolio you have, your recovery may be slow—and it may never happen. If you hold a well-diversified portfolio, you are sure to benefit from any market rebound. If you are heavily invested in a single market sector, you should eventually recoup your losses, but it could take decades. What if you own a handful of stocks? You may never recover your losses. Markets bounce back. Individual companies often die.

To get your portfolio back on track, try to think of

the stock market as both fairly valued and utterly random. The market tends to be fairly valued, meaning that it reflects all currently available information. Sure, there are always a few crooks running around, trading on inside information that the public doesn't know about. But most news, whether it is the company's latest earnings announcement, a change in an analyst's opinion on the stock, or news about the overall economy, gets reflected in a stock's price almost immediately. Result? If you sold all your stocks today, you would likely get prices that fairly accurately reflect the outlook for the companies involved.

But that doesn't mean that, if you waited a week, you wouldn't get prices that were substantially higher or significantly lower. News is coming out all the time. The market takes that news and quickly incorporates it into stock prices. That is what I mean by "utterly random." News, by its nature, is unpredictable. Maybe your stocks will rise because the news is good. Maybe they will fall because the news is bad. It is impossible to predict.

But whatever happens to your stocks, they are not going to rise or fall simply because they rose or fell last week or last year. The market doesn't care that you have lost a truckload of money. What the market cares about is what will happen next to a company's sales and earnings. If you are hanging onto an idiotic portfolio, held back by your reluctance to sell at a loss, you are making a huge mistake. If you can't bring yourself to recast your portfolio all at once, look to sell your losers gradually over the next year or 18 months. That way, if the stocks do bounce back, you will enjoy at least part of the rebound.

As an added bonus, selling will bring a pleasant tax

reward. If your losing stocks are held in a taxable account, you can use your losses to offset other capital gains and even ordinary income. Capital losses are first used to cancel out any capital gains. If you have further losses, they can be used to offset up to $3,000 in annual income. Do you have even more losses? You can carry those losses over to the next year and use them to reduce next year's taxes.

"I don't want to make it any worse." It is not just the "get even, then get out" syndrome that paralyzes investors. Another factor comes into play. What's that? As we lose money, we also lose confidence.

It seems that our cockiness tracks the market cycle. When stock prices rise, we become more self-assured, as we attribute our portfolio's gains to our own investment savvy. But when share prices slump, that confidence slips away. This rising and falling confidence shows up in trading among small investors. The longer a bull market lasts, the more investors trade, because they have the confidence to buy and sell. But when a bear market sets in, trading among small investors tends to slow, as investors grow increasingly unsure about what to do next.

This rising and falling confidence is also affected by the so-called house-money effect. Like casino gamblers who get lucky early in the evening, a bull market emboldens investors. We have made so much money that we feel that we can take a few extra risks in pursuit of higher returns. But as the bear market drags on, this cushion of gains shrivels and may disappear entirely, leaving us unwilling to risk further losses.

If you own a sensible portfolio, doing nothing isn't such a bad course of action. But with a little courage, you may be able to do even better. Falling markets create opportunities. In March 2000, investors were tripping over each other to buy stocks. Today, the water-cooler crowd has gone back to talking about fashion and football. The frenzy is long gone and the mob has fled, discarding stocks as they bolt for the exit. That doesn't mean that share prices are at bargain levels. But values are looking a whole lot more attractive.

"I knew it was a bubble." Kicking yourself for buying lousy stocks and losing funds? Your self-flagellation probably doesn't stop there. You may also be suffering from so-called hindsight bias. In retrospect, it seems obvious that the stock market was going to crash. Indeed, today many pundits talk about the market of the late 1990s as a bubble that inevitably burst.

In the late 1990s, share prices did get absurdly over-valued. Still, there was a lot of uncertainty about the market's direction. At the March 2000 market top, many market strategists were relentlessly bullish, many fund managers were fully invested in stocks, and many analysts were screaming, "Buy, buy, buy." On the day the S&P 500 peaked, over a billion shares were sold on the New York Stock Exchange. But a billion shares were also bought. Even in March 2000, after an astonishing bull market that had lasted almost 18 years, there were plenty of investors who were willing to bet that additional gains lay ahead. Not every investor thought a market crash was inevitable.

There is a good reason for that. The market crash

wasn't inevitable. While rich stock valuations made a severe decline more likely, what sent share prices spiraling lower was bad news, including the recession, September 11, and a slew of accounting scandals. And nobody—not the market strategists, not the television pundits, not your next-door neighbor—saw all that coming. The crash was not inevitable. You shouldn't berate yourself for not selling.

"It's headed for zero." Often, we take market trends and project them into the future. Seen stocks soar? Many investors assume that shares will keep on rising. As traders like to say, "The trend is your friend."

But the trend isn't always your friend. The same tendency to extrapolate returns kicks in during a market decline. Have stock prices been tumbling for a while? Soon enough, investors believe that further declines are inevitable. But this sort of thing is foolish. If you chase market trends, you will always be late to the party, buying after investments have booked great gains and selling after the losses have already piled up.

By 2002, the "headed-for-zero" crowd was crowing loudly. Stocks were dead, claimed anguished investors. Stocks are never coming back, they argued. As the drumbeat grew louder, many stock-fund holders abandoned hopes of getting back to even and instead hit the panic button. In July alone, a record $52.6 billion was pulled out of stock funds, according to the Investment Company Institute.

Nobody can predict what will happen to stocks over the next few years. But this much is clear: Many of the investors who abandoned stocks in 2002 didn't have to sell. They had ample time to ride out the market decline and book handsome gains in the decades ahead. But instead, they lost their nerve, locked in their losses, and gave up all chance of profiting from a market rebound.

"I'm not going to sit here and lose everything." Many investors may be paralyzed, afraid of compounding their earlier mistakes, reluctant to sell at a loss, and unsure of what to do next. But for another contingent, the sense of crisis brings with it an urge to act. But what are you going to do? Some people are loading up on bonds. Others are moving their stock-market money into real estate.

A smart move? Both real estate and bonds deserve a place in your portfolio. But betting everything on either one is absurd. Think about what investors did during the 1990s bull market. They bet everything on stocks. They made an all-or-nothing decision. That didn't work out so well. Yet here we are, a few years later, and many people are once again making all-or-nothing decisions. They are taking one ridiculously risky bet and replacing it with another.

Don't get me wrong. After the huge market decline, every investor should take a close look at his or her portfolio and most people will need to make at least some adjustments. But if you are going to avoid another debacle, you must shove aside the torrent of emotions. Forget freezing, or panicking, or acting impulsively. Instead, you need to behave as rationally as possible. Where to start? As a first step, spend a little time thinking about your financial goals.

FUNDING YOUR FUTURE

We save now so that we can spend later. But what will we spend our money on? Most families have at least four goals. They want to buy a decent home, send the kids to college, retire in comfort, and be prepared for financial emergencies. You may also have other financial goals. Maybe you want to buy a vacation home or trade up to a bigger house. Maybe you are hankering after a sports car or a boat. Maybe you are tired of long hours and high pressure, so you want to swap into a lower-paying and less-taxing job.

Whatever your goals, you probably can't afford your full financial wish list. But there is one goal you will have to be able to afford. You will have to retire. Yes, some people continue working into their seventies and even their eighties. But many companies push employees into retirement far earlier than that. And let's face it, most of us will be happy to go. We want to retire. We are tired of dragging ourselves out of bed every morning, hauling on the work clothes, and hustling out the door.

But retiring in comfort takes a ton of money. As a rule of thumb, you can generate $5,000 a year of pre-tax retirement income for every $100,000 you have saved. Add that to Social Security and any company pension you will receive and you can quickly get a handle on your likely retirement income. So how much have you got saved? If you are like the typical household, the piggy bank is almost empty. Consider some numbers from AARP, the Washington-based group for seniors. AARP calculates that, as of 1998, families headed by fifty- to sixty-one-year-olds had a median net worth of $127,600.

That figure includes home equity. Once you back that out, you find these households have just $70,600. That is enough to generate maybe $3,500 a year in retirement income. The bottom line? If these folks are lucky, they will receive both Social Security and a pension. If they are unlucky, they will have to rely on Social Security alone. But in either case, the typical household won't get a whole lot of retirement income from its portfolio. Have you seen your investments devastated by the stock-market crash? Here is a comforting thought: You are probably still better off than the typical household. After all, at least you have some sort of portfolio. A lot of people don't.

To rebuild your nest egg, you will need to sock away a slug of money. Yet saving money doesn't exactly rank among our more popular national pastimes. According to figures from the U.S. Department of Commerce, Americans saved an average of 6 percent a year of their disposable income in the 1990s, down from 9.1 percent in the 1980s, 9.6 percent in the 1970s, 8.3 percent in the 1960s, and 8 percent in the 1950s. But if the 1990s were grim, the current decade has been even worse, with the savings rate at 2.8 percent in 2000 and 2.3 percent in 2001, before improving modestly in early 2002.

Saving more for retirement doesn't just mean spending less. It also means scrimping on other financial goals. If your nest egg has been battered by the stock-market decline and you are far short of what you will need for retirement, it is time to make some tough choices. Maybe you can't have the sports car and the boat. Maybe you won't be able to retire early and maybe you shouldn't trade up to a bigger house. Maybe, in fact, you shouldn't pay for your children's college educations.

The latter suggestion might sound harsh. But it goes to a basic problem with saving and spending. We find it awfully tough to look ahead. We tend to fork over money now and figure the future will take care of itself. But if you want to retire in comfort, the ostrich approach won't work. You have to take care of the future now. Suppose you are far short of what you need for retirement. Nonetheless, you ignore the problem. You don't encourage your children to go to a less-expensive college. You don't ask them to take on college loans. Instead, you merrily cough up the money. The problem is, 25 years from now, you will be retired and the money will be running low.

What will you do? Will you ask your children for money, telling them that it is the least they can do, because you paid for their fine college educations? You lavished money on them and now you are asking for it back. The trouble is, they never knew it was a loan. They thought that it was a gift. Will they be a little angry that you made a major financial choice on their behalf? Yeah, believe me, they will be angry. Want to retire in comfort? By all means, help your children as much as you reasonably can. But if you really want to help them, you need to help yourself. Be smart about your finances today, so your kids won't have to bail you out tomorrow.

LOOKING ON THE BRIGHT SIDE

As you set out to rebuild your retirement nest egg, there is one piece of good news: The stock market has crashed. The cause of your agony is also the potential source of your salvation. The fact is, the collapse in share prices may end up bolstering your long-run wealth.

At the market peak in 2000, every dollar invested in stocks purchased an extraordinarily small claim on dividends and earnings. The market was so richly valued that the prospective long-run return from stocks was probably little better than that from bonds, and it may well have been worse. No doubt many investors would be thrilled to have share prices back at their bull-market peak. But if the market had stayed at its early 2000 level, people who bought stocks would have been severely disappointed with their returns over the next 10 years.

Instead, you now have the chance to do far better. We still aren't likely to see double-digit annual returns over the next 10 years. Nonetheless, stocks are a far more appealing proposition than they were three years ago. Many investors, of course, don't feel that way. They were wildly enthusiastic about the market when stocks were flying high, yet they have nothing but disdain now that share prices are so much lower. But this is all wrong. When the department stores hold their after-Christmas sales, shoppers rush to buy. When the market tumbles, investors should summon up the same bargain-hunting instinct.

But don't take my word on it. Instead, listen to Warren Buffett, chairman of Berkshire Hathaway and probably the market's most astute investor. "If you expect to be a net saver during the next five years, should you hope for a higher or lower stock market during that period?" asks Mr. Buffett in Berkshire Hathaway's 1997 annual report. "Many investors get this one wrong. Even though they are going to be net buyers of stocks for many years to come, they are elated when stock prices rise and depressed when they fall." A sentence later, he continues: "This reaction makes no sense. Only those who will be sellers of equities in the near future should be happy at seeing stocks rise. Prospective purchasers should much prefer sinking prices."

Thanks to the bear market, every dollar invested in stocks today buys more dividends and more earnings than a dollar invested three years ago. For anybody who regularly adds money to his or her stock portfolio or reinvests dividends, that is great news. You may have suffered huge short-term losses. But thanks to the higher gains now available on money invested and dividends reinvested, you should end up with greater long-run wealth and a more comfortable retirement.

For those who aren't investing fresh savings and reinvesting their dividends, the news isn't so cheery. Among investors, the hardest-hit group has been retirees who overdosed on stocks. If you are in this camp, you can't take advantage of the market decline by investing more money. Worse still, you may be forced to sell shares at depressed prices to cover living expenses. Nonetheless, there are strategies that can help you weather the decline and squeeze more income out of your battered portfolio. As you will discover in Chapter 7, the choices aren't always pleasant. But there are ways to salvage your nest egg and boost your retirement income. There is indeed hope.

2 LEARNING YOUR LESSON

The stock market has sent out some steep tuition bills over the past few years. But many investors, I fear, still haven't learned their lesson.

Ask your family, friends, and colleagues what insights they are taking away from three years of stock-market mayhem and you will likely hear all manner of answers. True, nobody spouts the nonsense of the late 1990s. You don't hear people talking about the New Economy, or how the Internet changed everything, or how earnings don't matter. That sort of foolishness is long gone.

But, unfortunately, the new investment mantras aren't a whole lot better, and that worries me. What investors choose to learn from the market collapse is critically important, because those lessons will guide our actions in the years ahead. Below, I have listed just some of the garbage you hear in the wake of the stock-market decline. My fear: As investors seek to rebuild their retirement nest eggs, they will latch onto one of these mantras and once again decimate their savings.

"Buy-and-hold doesn't work anymore." For years, investment experts have heaped scorn on market timing, the strategy of jumping in and out of stocks in an effort to catch bull markets and sidestep market declines. There is a good reason for this disdain. Stock-market forecasters exist to make astrologers look good. As these hapless gurus have proven over and over again, there is no reliable way of identifying market peaks and troughs.

Yet, ever fickle, Wall Street and ordinary investors are now embracing market timing. Partly, that reflects recent history. Over the past three years, holding stocks hasn't exactly been a joyous experience. But this newly found affection for market timing also reflects the hindsight bias mentioned in Chapter 1. In retrospect, it seems obvious that stocks were going to crash and that we all should have sold. The problem is, it wasn't at all obvious at the time. Even at the March 2000 peak, there were plenty of folks who thought that stocks still had further to run.

Planning to try your hand at market timing? You had better be pretty darn good, for two reasons. First, despite recent experience, stocks do rise over time. Any time you move money out of stocks and into more conservative investments, you are betting against this long-run upward trend. Stock-market history is littered with gurus who declared that stocks were set to collapse, only to see share prices soar even higher.

Second, it is difficult to succeed at market timing, once you factor in the costs involved. If you are not careful, you will rack up hefty brokerage commissions and other trading costs. Jumping in and out of stocks can also thoroughly mess up your tax return. If you sell a slug of stocks held in your taxable account, you will have to list all those trades on your tax return and pay taxes on any profits you make. There is, however, a silver lining: If you are a really bad market timer and you trade in your taxable account, you can use the resulting losses to reduce your annual tax bill.

Better still, forget market timing. So what should you do? I will talk more about portfolio building in the pages ahead, especially Chapters 6 and 7. But for now, take my word on it: Buy-and-hold is still your best long-run strategy.

"It's 1966 all over again." History doesn't repeat itself. Top-performing mutual funds often falter. Time-tested stock-picking strategies suddenly fail. Usually reliable market indicators start flashing red when they should be green.

But none of this seems to deter investors, who are constantly gazing back at earlier market cycles, picking out patterns in stock performance and then betting serious money that those patterns will repeat. Today, many investors reckon that we are in for a prolonged period of lousy stock returns. Their favorite historical analogy is the 1966–82 period. As stock-market bears will happily inform you, the Dow Jones Industrial Average in August 1982 was 22 percent lower than it was at the market peak in February 1966. That was over 16 years when stocks went nowhere.

But statistics like this don't tell the whole story. For starters, these raw averages reflect share-price changes but ignore dividends, which were then much higher. If you include those dividends, you find that the Standard & Poor's 500-stock index climbed 5.1 percent a year between 1966 and 1982. That is still pretty grim, especially compared to the 7 percent inflation rate. Other parts of the market fared far better, however, with small stocks earning 12.7 percent annually and foreign stocks gaining an estimated 9 percent a year. If you owned a globally diversified portfolio during this stretch, you wouldn't have gotten rich, but you would have kept ahead of inflation.

Moreover, as I mentioned in Chapter 1, dismal periods for the market can be great moneymakers if you invest regularly in stocks. By socking away $100 or $200 every month through rough patches, such as today's market or 1966–82, you can turn the misery of a market decline into a great opportunity to build long-run wealth.

When the bears aren't comparing today's stock market to 1966's, they are declaring that it is "Japan all over again." Supposedly, we are in for a grueling bear market in the decade ahead, comparable to the vicious stock-market decline suffered by the Japanese over the past 13 years. But this analogy is a stretch.

U.S. stocks never got as pricey as shares in Japan and we haven't had the accompanying collapse in real-estate prices that the Japanese endured. In addition, the U.S. banking system is far sounder than Japan's, government regulation is far less restrictive, and corporations are far more nimble. For U.S. stock prices to suffer a protracted decline, we would need protracted economic turmoil and possibly deflation, comparable to what the Japanese have suffered. Likely? I sure wouldn't bet on it.

"Small investors got what they deserved." Wall Street is forever decrying the stupidity of small investors. In fact, Wall Street is the only industry in America where it is considered good business practice to bad mouth the customer.

But this bashing of small investors is nothing more than another Wall Street marketing ploy. The stock-market collapse hurt everybody, professionals and amateurs alike. Small investors may have been heavily invested in stocks at the March 2000 stock-market peak. But so, too, were professionals.

Why does Wall Street delight in belittling small investors? As always, you have to follow the money. Wall Street's profits are far fatter when people invest through brokers and financial planners, rather than making their own investment decisions. The problem is, if you sign up with the typical high-cost adviser, you are almost guaranteed to garner mediocre returns.

I am not going to pretend that ordinary investors always make smart decisions. Some people do need an investment adviser. I will tell you how to find a good, low-cost adviser in the next chapter. But most folks, I believe, can invest successfully on their own. If you have a little intellectual curiosity and a healthy dose of emotional fortitude, building and maintaining a decent portfolio shouldn't prove too taxing. Moreover, if you are prudent, going the do-it-yourself route will almost certainly turn out to be more rewarding, because your performance won't be held back by hefty investment-advisory fees.

"Index funds are guaranteed mediocrity. Now, it's a stock picker's market." Even as Wall Street belittles your investment abilities, it also wants you to believe that you can beat the stock-market averages. This, of course, is contradictory. But it is also entirely self-serving. The more you trade and the more you invest with active money managers, the more money the Street makes.

Increasingly, some of the market's savviest investors

have turned their backs on this claptrap. They have given up on active managers who pursue market-beating returns and instead bought index funds, which simply seek to replicate the performance of a stock-market average while charging modest investment costs. In Chapter 3, I will discuss index funds further and explain why I think that they are a brilliant investment.

But Wall Street doesn't want you to buy index funds, because they aren't a particularly profitable product for the Street. Instead, Wall Street wants you to keep shooting for market-beating returns. That is why you should be suspicious when you hear talk of the supposed "stock picker's market." Brokers and market strategists often make this comment in flat and falling markets. The notion is that anybody can score decent profits in a bull market. But when stock prices are struggling, you need to select the right stocks to earn decent gains.

This advice may work for some investors. But it can't work for everyone. No matter what the direction of share prices, stock investors will still collectively earn the performance of the stock-market average. If one stock picker manages to select winning stocks, another stock picker must inevitably lag behind. In fact, once you figure in investment costs, most stock investors end up trailing behind the market average. A stock picker's market? It is just another piece of Wall Street gibberish.

"Stocks for the long run? I haven't got time for that nonsense." Jeremy Siegel, a finance professor at the University of Pennsylvania's Wharton School, wrote a fascinating book entitled *Stocks for the Long Run* that first appeared in 1994. The book noted that the stock market has been a remarkably reliable source of wealth, providing long-term investors with a return above inflation of some seven percentage points a year.

But as stocks have tumbled, that notion has been widely questioned. "Stocks for the long run" isn't yet a punch line on late-night television. But among bearish investors, the book's title is often mentioned with derision. All this is rather silly. In the 1990s, the New Era crowd seemed to believe that the market could only go up. Now, people seem to believe that stocks will never go up. Investors were wrong in the 1990s and they are wrong now.

As you will learn in the next chapter, I doubt that stocks will deliver as much as seven percentage points a year above inflation. Returns are likely to be somewhat lower in the decade ahead. But I am still a big proponent of stock-market investing. In fact, I am a lot more enthusiastic about stocks today than I was in March 2000. That enthusiasm grows with every market decline. What if the Dow Jones Industrial Average loses another 15 or 20 percent? I could become downright giddy.

"If you want steady gains, stick with bonds." Bonds were widely scorned in the 1990s, dismissed as the low-returning refuge of the timid and the terrified. Today, bonds could hardly be more popular. In 2002, the hunger for Treasury bonds was so great that the buying pressure drove yields down to levels not seen in four decades.

I think that you would be smart to include a healthy dose of bonds in your portfolio. But as you will discover in Chapter 4, I would advise steering clear of conventional Treasury bonds and instead favoring corporate bonds and inflation-indexed Treasury bonds. While bonds may not beat stocks over the next 10 years, their returns shouldn't be that much lower. That means you may not give up too much in performance by tilting your portfolio toward bonds. Nonetheless, bonds alone won't make you rich. Anybody who is bailing out of stocks and betting exclusively on bonds is making a huge mistake.

"You can't go wrong with real estate." Like bonds, real estate has become wildly popular in the wake of the market crash. A September 2002 poll found that 45 percent of those surveyed thought that real estate would outperform stocks over the next three years, while only 12 percent thought stocks would outperform. The survey was conducted by Opinion Research Corp. for Behringer Harvard Funds. By 2002, enthusiasm for real estate was so rampant that some commentators speculated that the stock-market bubble had been replaced by a bubble in real estate.

As with bonds, real estate deserves a prominent place in your portfolio. If you add together the likely price appreciation and potential income, you may be able to clock something close to double-digit gains with either rental properties or real-estate investment trusts. Still, some of the real-estate strategies being touted today will turn out to be big money losers. We will talk about those dubious strategies in Chapter 5.

MAKING THE GRADE

Investors may love to make money. But they also love to talk about making money. Turn on CNBC. Check out the Internet bulletin boards. Lean over the garden fence. You will hear all kinds of quirky financial theories, outlandish investment tips, and selectively edited stock-market war stories. And all this talk is just fine, just so long as you don't act on it. The problem, of course, is that many people do act. They get caught up in the daily market turmoil, they think they have some real market insight, and they end up making the craziest investments.

I, too, love to talk about investing. I find the market utterly fascinating. Every trading day is packed with drama, as stocks climb on rumors, the market shudders with the latest political development, and companies are punished for failing to deliver the expected earnings. But in the end, I view this stuff as just entertainment. It is noise. It is nothing more than an amusing distraction from the serious business of making money. But in many ways, it is a necessary distraction, because sensible investing is so darn simple and so darn boring. This stuff is not rocket science.

Which brings us to the lessons of the stock-market decline. What should we make of the great market debacle? Ignore the blather emanating from the television, the newspaper, and the other side of the garden fence. Ignore the "new" investment wisdom about buy-and-hold being dead, about index funds being guaranteed mediocrity, and about how you can't go wrong with real estate.

The past three years do indeed have much to teach

us. But what they reinforce is the value of certain time-tested investment ideas. Want to make sure that you don't flunk out all over again? Want to ensure that you can retire on time? I will talk about some of the bear market's more-specific lessons in the chapters ahead. But here, I believe, are the three crucial principles that have been highlighted by the market decline and that should guide your investing in the years ahead.

LESSON NO. 1: WE ARE THE ENEMY

The market may have misbehaved over the past three years. But the market always misbehaves. We have, without a doubt, lived through a terrible stock-market decline. But the decline wasn't unprecedented. In 2002, stocks suffered their third losing year in a row. But that has happened before. The S&P 500 posted three consecutive losses between 1939 and 1941 and it had four losing years between 1929 and 1932.

The problem isn't the market. Rather, the problem is investors. In the late 1990s, our expectations got out of whack with reality. Rapidly rising stock prices should have made investors nervous about future returns. But instead, the market's steady climb made folks increasingly comfortable with stocks. Bear markets became a distant memory and people were banking on 20 percent annual gains every year. Investors should have been mentally prepared for a market crash. But they weren't.

For many investors, today's market carnage shouldn't matter. If you are fifty years old, you can reasonably expect to live to age eighty-five, and you might live to ninety-five or beyond. Your time horizon is 35 years and possibly longer. The biggest obstacle to a bright financial future isn't the market's short-run gyrations, but the long-run threat posed by inflation and taxes. Historically, stocks have been a great way to stave off those threats.

But at times like this, such notions are scant comfort. Our investment time horizon might be 30 or 40 years. Our emotional time horizon, however, sometimes stretches no further than the end of the trading day. Our investment outlook, not to mention our sense of well-being, starts to hinge on every stock-market twitch.

It is no great surprise that real estate and bonds are suddenly the favored investments. With bonds, you get a predictable stream of income. With real estate, the bricks and mortar are there in front of your eyes. But what do you get when you buy a stock? It is far more nebulous. You might collect a small dividend. But the real value lies in a company's ability to generate profits. When you purchase a stock, you are buying a piece of a corporation and laying claim to a sliver of all its future earnings. As those earnings rise, the company's stock price will climb and its ability to pay dividends will increase.

But rather than focusing on dividends and earnings, investors let their sense of value be determined by what the market says. This is craziness. Suppose you were told every day what your house was worth. Would you panic and sell because you suddenly discovered that your home was worth $25,000 less than you expected? Probably not. You would likely conclude that your house still provided a perfectly decent place to live and that today's price was irrelevant, because you didn't intend to sell for many years.

You need to adopt a similar attitude not just with

stocks, but with your entire investment strategy. All this fretting isn't fun and it doesn't help. Want to be a successful and happy investor? Yes, you need to settle on strategies that will allow you to retire in comfort. But that alone isn't enough. You also need an investment plan that you will have faith in, no matter how rough the market gets.

LESSON NO. 2: KEEP IT SIMPLE

With the stock market in a funk, investors have been flailing around, trying to find new ways to milk money out of stocks. You hear that buying and holding prosaic mutual funds is no longer a smart strategy. Instead, you need to sell stocks short, or write covered call options, or time the market, or hire a private money manager, or sign on with a hedge-fund manager.

I am not going to explain all of these supposedly sophisticated strategies. But isn't this where we got into trouble in the first place? In the 1990s, mutual funds were also dismissed as dull investments. Instead, investors got way too clever, flipping initial public stock offerings, buying stocks on margin, day trading, and betting heavily on technology stocks, especially dicey Internet companies.

But as they say on Wall Street, when the tide goes out, you find out who is swimming naked. It is clear that many people neither fully understood the companies they were buying nor fully appreciated the risks they were taking. They pursued cutting-edge strategies, and they ended up getting sliced and diced.

Why are we such sluts for sophistication? Investors often assume that if an investment smacks of complexity or exclusivity, it is somehow superior. And that is just what Wall Street wants you to believe. But the truth is, "complexity," "sophistication," and "exclusivity" are usually excuses for Wall Street to charge fat fees.

Consider hedge funds. The funds have lately been in vogue, because they often perform well when stocks don't. These "uncorrelated returns" stem from the strategies used. For instance, a market-neutral hedge fund might simultaneously go both "long" and "short," buying stocks it likes, while betting against those that appear overvalued. If the hedge fund holds an equal amount of long and short bets, its results will be driven by the relative performances of those bets, rather than by the performance of the overall stock market.

But while this may sound clever, it is also mighty expensive. All that trading isn't cheap. Hedge funds also typically charge money-management fees equal to 1 percent of assets each year, plus snagging 20 percent of any profits above a specified hurdle rate. In addition, many investors end up paying another layer of money-management fees, because they purchase a "fund of funds." With a fund of funds, what you get is an investment pool that tries to make money by investing in a variety of hedge funds.

All these costs might seem reasonable if good performance was assured. But it isn't. Hedge funds have cultivated a reputation as the ultimate in "smart money" and as the favored investment vehicle of the superrich. But it turns out that the returns are nothing to write home about.

For instance, a study by hedge-fund managers Clifford Asness, Robert Krail, and John Liew found that hedge funds lagged behind the S&P 500 by roughly seven percentage points a year between January 1994 and September 2000. The study, which appeared in the Fall 2001 *Journal of Portfolio Management,* also found that many hedge funds tended to perform like the broad market and thus they weren't the great diversifiers they claim to be.

But awkward facts like these never stopped Wall Street's marketing machines. Sensing a chance to make a quick buck, the Street in 2002 began flogging hedge funds to less-affluent investors. Instead of demanding the usual minimum of $1 million or more, money-management firms have rolled out hedge funds with minimums of just $50,000. Fortunately, on this occasion, there is a limit to how many sheep the Street can fleece. Despite the lower price of admission, hedge funds are still out of reach for most investors, because the funds aren't legally allowed to accept you as a customer unless you have a hefty amount of other assets.

The bottom line: Hedge funds, like so many other cutting-edge investments, just don't live up to their billing. It is time to ditch our obsession with sophistication. Investing is best when it is simplest. Why? There are two reasons. First, simple investments typically involve lower expenses. That gives you a big advantage over most other investors, whose results are often dragged down by hefty investment costs.

Second, if you buy simple investments that you fully understand, you are less likely to be unpleasantly surprised and you are more likely to tough it out at times of turmoil. In the 1990s, many investors didn't understand the technology companies they were buying. Given that lack of knowledge, it is hardly surprising that so many people panicked when share prices turned against them.

Similarly, I fear that there will be rough days ahead for many folks who today are investing in hedge funds, writing covered call options, buying real estate, and "shorting" stocks in a bet that those stocks will decline. These people don't fully understand what they are doing. Result: When times turn tough, they are likely to turn tail.

So what should you buy? Forget Wall Street's exotic garbage. Instead, stick with stock, bond, and money-market funds. Mutual funds are simple to understand. That understanding will give you faith in your strategy, thus reducing the likelihood of self-inflicted investment wounds. With a handful of low-cost mutual funds, you can build a top-flight portfolio. Your portfolio may not make Wall Street rich. But it should generate more than enough money for you.

LESSON NO. 3: HUMILITY RULES

I am a big fan of mutual funds. But mutual funds are no panacea. There are plenty of funds that delivered dreadful results over the past three years. Clearly, you want to own the right funds. But which are the right funds? This is where we run into our most-persistent enemy, over-confidence. Most investors end up with mediocre investment results. Yet many folks believe that they can succeed, even as others fail. This overconfidence isn't a bad trait. Optimistic, confident people tend to be happier than other folks. They cope better with stress. They are more likely to succeed at their chosen profession.

The problem is, our copious self-confidence also means that we overestimate our chances of winning, even when the outcome depends on luck. In fact, in such situations, the people who have the most realistic outlook aren't the folks who are optimistic and self-confident. Instead, according to psychologists, the people who have the most realistic assessment tend to be those who are mildly or severely depressed. These folks, it seems, are quicker to concede that certain situations are beyond their control.

What about the rest of us? Faced with the chaotic, uncontrollable financial markets, we still believe that we can control our destiny and come out ahead. This excessive self-confidence, so helpful in other parts of our life, is a real handicap when it comes to investing. It encourages us to trade too much. It encourages us to make hefty, undiversified bets on stocks, or bonds, or real estate. It encourages us to believe that we know far more about future returns than we really do.

Buoyed by excessive self-confidence, investors loaded up on technology funds in the late 1990s and early 2000, only to see their wealth shredded by the market decline. Undaunted, they are at it again, betting today on bonds and real estate. I don't know whether these bets will also blow up. But I do know that these investors are taking an unnecessary risk. Indeed, they are taking a risk that most of them can ill afford. Remember the brutal math of investing? If you lose 25 percent, you need a 33 percent gain to get back to even. If you lose 50 percent, you need a 100 percent gain to recoup your investment losses. If you surrender 75 percent, it takes a 300 percent gain to get your money back.

The bigger the hit, the harder it is to recover. So who suffers the big hits? Those who make big bets. So what is the lesson? You've got it: Stop making big, stupid, bonehead bets. It is time for a little humility. It is time to concede that you don't know which investment will be the next big winner. It is time to diversify, spreading your money across stocks, bonds, and real estate, across a fistful of market sectors, across a truckload of individual securities. There is no one right fund. Instead, you need to own a lot of funds, each of which will give you exposure to a different part of the global market. If you diversify like this, you can still earn great returns, but the risk involved is much reduced.

This risk reduction shows up in three ways. First, by investing across a slew of individual securities, you avoid getting wiped out if any one company gets into financial trouble, prompting its bonds to nosedive and its shares to go into a tailspin.

Second, if you diversify, you can reduce the risk of dramatically underperforming the market average. Thanks to a popular Wall Street rule of thumb, many people underestimate how many stocks they need to own to be well diversified. According to the rule of thumb, you need just 15 or 20 stocks to build a decently diversified stock portfolio. With that many stocks, you may be protected against any one company going bust.

But that still leaves the problem of tracking error. If you own just 20 stocks, you could easily lag behind the market by two or more percentage points a year. Over time, that seemingly small annual hit can make a massive difference to your ultimate wealth. Want to eliminate tracking error? You need to own not 20 stocks, but hundreds and hundreds of companies. The only practical way to do that is through mutual funds.

Third, diversification smoothes a portfolio's year-to-year performance. Investments don't rise and fall in lockstep. When stocks are getting battered, bonds may post healthy gains. When blue-chip stocks are underwater, foreign shares may come to the rescue. Diversification allows you to combine the wildest of securities and end up with a relatively tame investment mix, as losses in one part of your portfolio are offset by gains elsewhere.

For instance, you would need an extraordinarily strong stomach to invest only in gold stocks or only in emerging markets. But if you take a well-diversified portfolio and add a small position in these investments, you can actually reduce the portfolio's overall risk.

Similarly, an all-bond portfolio might seem less risky than any investment mix that includes stocks. But as it turns out, a mix of 80 percent bonds and 20 percent stocks is no riskier than an all-bond portfolio, but its expected return is much higher. How can the 80 percent bond–20 percent stock portfolio be no more risky? Bonds don't always make money. When your bonds are suffering, your stocks may post gains, thus smoothing out your portfolio's overall performance.

Diversification doesn't just reduce risk. It can also make you a more-tenacious investor. Because your portfolio will perform less erratically, you are more likely to stick with your investments through times of turmoil. Want to build a portfolio that you will have confidence in? Diversification, like simplicity, can help to give you the necessary faith. When the market crashes, some stocks will never recover. But a well-diversified portfolio will eventually rebound. That knowledge should bolster your resolve.

Diversification, however, isn't a cure-all. Underlying the notion is a big assumption, which is that you will focus on your portfolio's performance, rather than fret about each investment you own. But in reality, you may gnash your teeth over individual investments, even if your overall portfolio is doing just fine. Diversification may give you greater faith in your portfolio. But you will still have your queasy moments.

If you have suffered big losses, the whole idea of diversifying may be difficult to stomach. You know that you have a lopsided portfolio, with too little in bonds and too much in technology shares or too much in your employer's stock. You would rather be diversified. But you are reluctant to make the move now. What if technology stocks rebound strongly? What if your employer's shares suddenly rocket higher? Not only will you miss out on those gains, but also you will feel just dreadful.

This is a tough one. But I would argue that there is never a bad time to diversify. Just because technology stocks are deeply underwater doesn't mean that they will come roaring back. There is no way of knowing which part of the market will do best in the years ahead. Performance is unpredictable. But this much is certain: If you diversify, you will undoubtedly reduce your portfolio's risk.

Put that way, it seems clear what investors should do. Stop betting on something as uncertain as a big rebound in technology stocks. Instead, go for the sure thing. Go for the certainty of reduced risk by building yourself a well-diversified portfolio that includes stocks, bonds, and real estate.

To be sure, every year, there will be another hot sector and you will wish you had invested more in those stocks. At times, holding a well-diversified portfolio will seem foolish, as parts of your portfolio take big short-term hits. But trust me: Over the long haul, diversifying is one decision most investors never regret.

3 RESTOCKING YOUR PORTFOLIO

Looking back at early 2000, it might seem as though investors' biggest mistake was overloading on stocks, especially technology shares. But the error was more basic than that. Investors fundamentally misunderstood the game.

What game? Welcome to the greatest of investment fantasies: You can beat the stock market. At the end of the previous chapter, I argued the case for humility. Don't bet everything on stocks, or bonds, or real estate. Instead, you ought to diversify, owning some of each. But the need for humility doesn't stop there. It is also time to abandon the dangerous pursuit of stock-market–beating returns.

Make no mistake: It is indeed dangerous. Investors spend billions every year trying to win the stock-market game, only to find themselves falling even further behind the market average. The reality is, very few people manage to beat the market. Reams of statistics prove this. For instance, over the 30 years through year-end 2001, stock mutual funds returned an average 10.7 percent a year, versus 12.2 percent for the Standard & Poor's 500-stock index, according to calculations by the Vanguard Group using Lipper data.

But who needs statistics? Simple logic will do the trick. Investors, as a group, cannot beat the market, because collectively we are the market. Throw in investment costs and investors collectively are destined to lag behind the market average. This isn't a matter of debate. It is incontrovertible logic.

FEEDING THE FANTASY

The beat-the-market fantasy may be dangerous and absurd. But it is also highly profitable—for Wall Street. Brokerage houses and money-management firms thrive on the fantasy. They need people to trade like crazy and to buy actively managed stock funds that gun for market-beating returns. Wall Street's profitability hinges on investors believing the fantasy. But what about the incontrovertible logic? What about the damning statistics? Wall Street shrugs off such inconvenient facts.

Instead, like a clever con man, it keeps the beat-the-market fantasy alive through razzle-dazzle, sleight of hand, and the gullibility of investors. It starts with a single-minded focus on the market's winners. Money-management companies advertise their top-performing stock funds. Newsletters tout their winning records. Brokerage firms boast of their research departments' stock-picking prowess.

The results involved are often astonishingly good. But this is no great surprise. If you have enough monkeys throwing darts, some of the primates are bound to hit the bull's-eye. If you have enough investors trying to beat the market, some will inevitably get lucky and outpace the index.

Not only are there bound to be some winners, but some of these winners will also post huge gains, thanks to an intriguing statistical quirk. The most a stock can lose is 100 percent. But the potential gain is unlimited. This "skewness" heavily influences stock-market returns. In any given year, there is often a fistful of stocks that post outrageously large gains.

This has a perverse effect. To observers who see these huge gains, it seems like stocks offer an easy way to get rich quick. But when these observers try to pick winners themselves, they usually end up lagging behind the market average.

That, however, is exactly what you would expect. Because the big winners perform so well, they tend to drag up the results of the market average, so that a majority of stocks end up trailing behind this average. Just bought one or two stocks? The odds suggest that these companies will be among the majority of stocks that lag behind the market average.

Your chances of beating the market become even smaller, once you figure in trading costs, mutual-fund fees, and other investment expenses. Never forget the incontrovertible logic. Before costs, investors will match the results of the market average. After costs, investors will collectively lag behind. In fact, investors will collectively lag behind the market by a sum equal to their investment costs.

This mathematical truism might seem problematic for brokerage houses and money-management firms. If Wall Street is to make a ton of money, it will have to come at the expense of investors. Every extra dollar that the Street collects means that investors trail even further behind the market average. In essence, the interests of investors and the interests of Wall Street are diametrically opposed.

But the folks on Wall Street aren't stupid. Even as brokerage houses and money-management firms try to keep the focus on performance, they do their best to disguise the true costs of investing. Think about how Wall Street collects its cut. Mutual-fund annual expenses are silently deducted throughout the year. Asset-management fees are quietly subtracted each quarter. Trading costs eat into our returns without our ever noticing.

Costs aren't just hidden. They are also made to look small. Mutual-fund expenses, fund sales commissions, and asset-management fees aren't expressed as a percentage of your likely return. Brokers don't say, "I'm taking 20 percent of your potential gain." Instead, costs are expressed as a percentage of the total amount invested, which makes the sum appear a whole lot smaller. Not surprisingly, many investors don't realize how much they are paying and thus they don't fully appreciate how unlikely it is that they will beat the market.

While Wall Street is the great con man, the media seems to be the Street's loyal sidekick. Turn on CNBC. Flip through *Money* magazine. Read your local newspaper's business section. What you find is a seemingly relentless focus on hot stocks, short-term market performance, high-flying initial public stock offerings, dazzling hedge funds, and star mutual-fund managers.

The coverage may not be quite as breathless as it was three years ago. But there is still a giddiness to it all. You can't sell 12 issues a year of *Money* magazine by running headlines that read, "Five Ways to Build a Prudent, Well-Diversified Portfolio." You can't get people to read *The Wall Street Journal* every morning and watch CNBC every evening by saying, "Yeah, stocks were down again, but that's just statistical noise and now, once again, let's take a look at the long-run performance of the stock-market averages."

Faced with such a flood of misinformation, it is hardly surprising that novice investors try to beat the market. But in this great con, even veteran investors are often willing victims. Partly, it is overconfidence. We think we are smarter than others. But are we? Consider a study by Brad Barber and Terrance Odean that appeared in the April 2000 *Journal of Finance.*

The two finance professors looked at stock trading by individual investors who had accounts at a large discount-brokerage firm. Over the six-year stretch that they studied, Messrs. Barber and Odean found little difference between the precost returns of those who traded the most and those who traded the least. But after costs, the difference in performance was stunning. The confident, high-trading investors earned 11.4 percent a year, while the more-cautious, low-trading investors scored 18.5 percent. Meanwhile, the market climbed 17.9 percent annually.

After a while, experience ought to dent our confidence. It should dawn on us that all the trading is hurting our investment results and that our stock-fund managers are trailing the market average. But the truth is, most of us don't have a clue how our portfolio is really performing, so it is easy to delude ourselves. Studies suggest that investors consistently guess too high both when estimating their own past returns and also when predicting performance for the years ahead.

What happens when we can't hide from our losses anymore? We fall back on mental games. Had a bad year in 2002? We will simply write the year off. Bought some bum mutual funds? We will blame that on our broker. Picked a stock that cratered? As long as we hang onto the shares, it is just a "paper loss." And when we do finally get disgusted and sell, what do we do? Now that it is out of our portfolio, we won't count it in our performance calculations.

PAYING THE PIPER

There are plenty of people who still believe the fantasy. And for that, we should be grateful. These active investors ensure that stocks are efficiently priced and they provide "liquidity," giving us somebody to trade with next time we need to buy or sell stocks. These people are, without a doubt, providing a valuable service. But in most cases, it is also costing them dearly. Struggling to amass enough for retirement? I am not sure that you can afford to be so generous.

Why not? First, as I indicated above, attempts to beat the market hold the seeds of their own destruction, because these efforts are so darn expensive. Second, even if you keep costs down, these market-beating efforts can be extraordinarily risky.

Let's start with the question of costs. Suppose you try to beat the market average by trading individual stocks. That isn't a cheap undertaking. Seen all those advertisements from discount-brokerage firms, touting commissions of just $7 or $8 a trade? Tote up the full costs involved and you find that trading is a lot more expensive than that.

Not only will you pay a brokerage commission every time you buy and sell, but also your results will be trimmed by the bid–ask spread. While you see just one stock price in the newspaper, every stock actually has two prices: the higher price at which you can buy and the lower price at which you can sell. Thus, if you simultaneously bought and sold the same stock, you would lose money. The difference between the buy and sell prices represents the profit earned by the stock's market maker. There is a good chance that you will surrender more to the bid–ask spread than you lose to brokerage commissions.

If you trade large blocks of stock or you dabble in thinly traded shares, you may also incur "market impact" costs. Your own buying can propel a stock higher and your selling may drive the price lower, thus making it more expensive to trade the stock in question.

Finally, if you do a lot of trading in your taxable account, not only will you mess up your tax return, but also you will realize your stock-market profits quickly. That means that you will turn over a hefty chunk of your annual gains to Uncle Sam, resulting in lower after-tax performance.

If trading individual stocks seems expensive, hiring a fund manager can be equally costly. On average, stock funds charge around 1.5 percent of assets per year, plus losing maybe 0.5 percent a year to trading costs, including commissions, spreads, and market-impact costs. That means that fund managers have to beat the market by some two percentage points a year, just to keep even with the market average.

Mutual-fund statistics can be a little tricky, because fund-management companies tend to kill off funds with rotten results, usually merging these lousy performers into funds with better records. If you add back these rotten funds, you find that over long periods funds underperform the market by around 1.5 percentage points a year. In other words, it seems that funds do manage to earn back part of their investment costs, but their stock picking isn't nearly good enough to justify the fees they charge. If you purchase actively managed stock funds, you should expect to trail behind the stock-market average.

This laggardly performance can cost you big dollars over time. Suppose you invested $10,000 in a fund that notched 8.5 percent a year, while the market returned 10 percent. Over 20 years, your $10,000 would grow to $51,120. By contrast, if your money had simply mimicked the market's performance, it would have grown to $67,275. Moreover, fund performance looks even worse once you figure in both taxes and also the sales commissions charged by many funds.

Of course, if you are careful, you could keep costs low even as you try to beat the market. For instance, there are actively managed stock funds that don't charge a sales commission and that have annual expenses below 0.5 percent a year. Alternatively, in an effort to beat the market, you might pursue a low-cost strategy of simply buying and holding a handful of carefully chosen stocks. But unfortunately, even if you minimize investment costs, you still face another key problem: Trying to beat the market inevitably involves additional risk.

To outpace the stock-market average, you have to hold a portfolio that doesn't look like the market. Maybe you will bank heavily on particular stocks, overweight some sectors, buy actively managed funds, or flit between stocks and bonds as you bet on the stock market's direction. All these strategies can lead to market-beating results. But there is also a risk that your performance will be significantly worse than the stock-market average.

This risk wouldn't be a problem if there were sure-fire strategies for beating the market. But there aren't. It is one of the ironies of investing. The questions that intrigue us most (Which are the next hot stocks? Where is the market headed next? Which are the next superstar funds?) are the ones we are least capable of answering. There is no guaranteed way of beating the market.

True, there are strategies and funds that have generated dazzling results in the past. Picking last year's winners is easy. Forecasting next year's winners is a tad trickier. How are we going to select those winners? In other aspects of our lives, if we work hard, we usually get rewarded. What if we spend our weekends studying stocks and mutual funds? Surely we will know something that others don't and thus maybe we can beat the market? It seems so logical that this should be the case. And, yet, it is not.

Wall Street likes to present the market as a puzzle that we can all solve, if only we have enough smarts and enough help. But we are not solving a puzzle. We are trading with each other. We can all make money. But we can't all beat the market. Next time you buy or sell a stock, take a moment to consider who is on the other side of the trade. That person might have an MBA. She could be a professional money manager. He may be a senior executive at the company that issued the stock. Do you really know more than these other folks?

With all these smart people trading with one another, the result is all too predictable. As investors buy and sell shares based on their best guesses of what each company is worth, stocks end up trading at prices that fairly accurately reflect their underlying value, so it is enormously difficult to earn superior returns, especially once you figure in the investment costs involved. It is a battle of street-savvy gladiators that leaves most participants battered and bloodied, with nothing to show for their efforts but a costly, frustrating draw.

Admittedly, in any given year, it doesn't look like a draw. There are always winners. But can you be confident that the winners will keep on winning? If you have 5,000 coin flippers gathered in a stadium, the odds suggest that 156 will flip heads five times in a row. The successful coin flippers might claim that they are skillful. But we know that it was just luck.

Ditto for fund managers. Some will put together impressive 5- and even 10-year records. But are these records really that impressive? Maybe not. After all, as a matter of probability, you would expect there to be a fair number of big winners. But as with our coin flippers, it could just be luck. In fact, the history of the mutual-fund business is littered with spectacular failures—managers who topped the performance charts, were hailed as stock-picking geniuses, and then promptly crashed and burned.

You still want to try beating the market? You had better hope that you are one of the lucky few, because shooting for market-beating returns involves an extremely unattractive wager. You are risking the high probability of failure for the slim chance of superior returns. After the market losses of the past three years, can you really afford another failure?

If you save diligently and earn whatever the market delivers, you will likely retire in reasonable comfort. But what if you ignore the odds and keep gunning for market-beating returns? If you succeed, your retirement might be a little more comfortable. But what if you fail? What if you garner results that are far worse than the market average? Let's be honest: It doesn't bear thinking about.

PLAYING FOR NICKELS

Trying to beat the market almost always hurts. But it didn't seem to hurt that much in the 1990s. All the investment costs involved meant that you probably lagged behind the stock-market average. But the raw results were so high that even market-lagging performance meant pretty fat gains.

In all likelihood, the current decade won't be nearly so rewarding. As a result, if you rack up hefty costs in your efforts to beat the market, you could find yourself making little or no money. It is impossible to predict the stock market's short-run performance. But you can make a stab at forecasting returns over the next decade by looking at the three components of stock-market performance:

■ First, there is the dividend yield, which is the cash return you get every year. Occasionally, companies will cut or suspend their dividends, so you shouldn't bank on receiving the dividend from any one stock. But if you own a whole host of companies, dividends can provide a reliable and growing stream of income.

■ Second, there is the growth in corporate earnings. Those rising earnings will tend to drive share prices higher. But earnings and share prices don't move in lockstep. Why not? Much also depends on what happens to stock-market valuations.

■ The value put on stocks is reflected in our third factor, the market's share-price–to–earnings multiple, or P/E in Wall Street parlance. What's that? If a company's shares are at $40 and its earnings per share were $2 for the prior 12 months, then its stock would have a P/E of 20. Even if a company's earnings climb at a brisk pace, shareholders could still lose money if the stock's P/E multiple contracts. Historically, stocks have traded at an average of 15 times earnings. But in recent years, the overall stock market's P/E multiple has been much higher than that.

You can take these three components and use them to analyze the stock market's historical performance. According to a study by Roger Ibbotson and Peng Chen of Chicago's Ibbotson Associates, stocks climbed at over 10 percent a year since 1925. But how did we end up with that 10-percent–plus performance? According to the study, which appeared in the January/February 2003 *Financial Analysts Journal,* 4.3 percentage points came from dividends, 4.9 percentage points came from growth in earnings per share, and 1.3 points came from the rise in the stock market's P/E multiple. Meanwhile, inflation ran at 3.1 percent a year.

Now, consider where we stand today. Even after the recent bear market, stocks boast far higher P/E multiples than they did at the end of 1925. But this isn't particularly surprising. Seven decades ago, the world was a much more precarious place. For a study that appeared in the June 1999 *Journal of Finance,* professors William Goetzmann and Philippe Jorion looked at the fate of 24 national markets dating back to at least 1931.

During the years that followed, only seven markets, including the U.S., enjoyed uninterrupted trading. What happened to the other 17 markets? They were all at least temporarily shut down, typically resulting in huge stock-market losses. Many of these stock-market closings occurred during the Second World War.

We look back at the U.S. market's rise, and it seems as though stocks were a sure road to wealth. But in reality, there were doubts all along the way. Think about the perils that the U.S. faced. The Great Depression of the 1930s might have destroyed capitalism. The U.S. could have ended up on the losing side of the Second World War. The U.S. stock market could have been wiped out, like other national markets were.

In investing, to earn high returns, you have to take hefty risks. Over the past seven decades, U.S. stock investors took hefty risks, for which they were handsomely rewarded. Investors in many other markets weren't so lucky. They also took hefty risks, but their reward wasn't nearly so lavish.

Today, we might face terrorist attacks and economic recessions. But we clearly live in a more stable world. That is good news for society, but bad news for investors who are looking for double-digit stock returns. Over the past seven decades, as people came to view the world as a safer place, the market's price–earnings multiple climbed, adding 1.3 percentage points a year to stock returns. But this revaluation of stocks is probably over. It is doubtful that we will get a further big climb in the market's P/E multiple.

Similarly, in the years ahead, we are unlikely to get a whole lot of help from dividends. As share prices have climbed since 1925, dividends have shrunk as a percentage of stock prices. Instead of collecting 4.3 percentage points a year, as we have historically, today the market's dividend yield is around 2 percent.

Where does that leave us? If we are to enjoy decent stock-market gains, we must bank on growth in earnings per share. On that front, Wall Street is way too bullish. You will often hear 7 or even 10 percent annual earnings growth described as normal, with the prospect that carefully selected companies can do even better.

But, unfortunately, corporate America's track record isn't nearly so glowing. Since 1925, earnings per share have grown at 4.9 percent a year, or just 1.8 percentage points a year faster than inflation. That number is just astonishingly low. Can we do better than that in the years ahead? There is a ton of debate on this question, with the arguments centering on two key issues.

First, over the long haul, profits should grow at about the same clip as the economy. For instance, if the economy grows three percentage points a year faster than inflation, then you would expect profits to grow at a similar pace. But, unfortunately, things aren't that straightforward. Even if overall earnings expand as fast as the economy, growth in earnings per share will be somewhat slower, as companies issue new stock.

This is the reason you should be so alarmed when

you hear about management gorging itself on stock options. What that means is that the number of shares outstanding is likely to increase, so that earnings per share will grow more slowly than aggregate earnings. Management is effectively snagging part of the company at the expense of outside shareholders, who will see their stake diluted.

There is an additional reason that we could see earnings per share grow more slowly than the overall economy. It could be that, while the economy is expanding at a decent pace, the really fast growth isn't occurring among companies listed on the stock market. Instead, it may be that private companies are enjoying the truly spectacular growth, while shareholders of publicly traded companies are stuck with slower-growing corporations.

The second big source of debate focuses on whether companies will put retained earnings to good use. Historically, management has paid out over half of earnings as dividends. But today, on average, companies only pay out about a third of their profits. What do they do with the rest of the money? There are a bunch of uses. Management can buy back shares, thereby boosting growth in earnings per share and offsetting the effect of any new share issuance. They can plow the money back into the business. They can acquire other businesses. All of these strategies can lead to faster earnings growth.

But will they? Some commentators argue that, in the past, corporate executives have proved to be inept at investing retained earnings. Their contention: Today's managers are likely to be equally incompetent. I have some sympathy with this argument. Corporate executives, like investors, tend to be overly optimistic. All investors can't beat the market. Similarly, all companies can't grow faster than the economy. Many companies, which today are using earnings to pursue faster profit growth, would serve their shareholders far better by paying fatter dividends or buying back stock.

Where does all this leave us? I tend to split the difference, being neither as pessimistic as the bears nor as bullish as Wall Street's strategists and analysts. I figure stocks might, on average, deliver 8 percent a year over the next decade. How do I get that forecast? Earnings per share might rise three percentage points a year faster than inflation. That means that, if we get 3 percent inflation, profits would climb 6 percent annually. If we get 6 percent earnings growth and the market's price–earnings multiple remains the same, then share prices would also advance at 6 percent a year. Throw in 2 percent for dividends and we could see annual returns for the S&P 500 of 8 percent.

Thin gruel? I would disagree. We are talking about notching five percentage points a year faster than inflation, not too much below the 200-year average of 6.9 points, as calculated by Jeremy Siegel for the 2002 edition of his book, *Stocks for the Long Run.*

That crude estimate comes with three caveats. First, the return on a globally diversified portfolio could be somewhat higher. Smaller U.S. companies and foreign markets aren't as richly valued as blue-chip U.S. stocks, so folks who diversify beyond the S&P 500 may enjoy better performance. Second, we have been discussing raw market results. After costs, you will be left with less money in your pocket. Still, I figure that if you pay careful attention to costs and if you diversify globally, you should be able to collect 8 percent a year over the decade ahead.

Finally, and most critically, the return over the next decade could be much higher or lower if the market's price–earnings multiple climbs or contracts. But it is all but impossible to predict what will happen to P/Es. The stock market's P/E multiple tends to climb when interest rates fall, when economic growth picks up, and when investors are bullish. Conversely, rising interest rates, bad economic news, and investor uncertainty can cause P/Es to contract.

As stock prices tumbled during 2002, the chances improved that P/Es might expand in the future, so that stocks would deliver more than 8 percent a year. But if we do see any expansion in P/E multiples, it is likely to come early in the next bull market. Coming off the bottom of major bear markets, stocks often post explosive gains. Indeed, in the 12 months after the bottom of each of the past 12 bear markets, stocks gained an average 32.5 percent, according to SEI Investments in Oaks, Pennsylvania.

There is a decent chance that we will see similar gains during the first year of the next bull market. But once that spurt has passed, investors will be back to relying on earnings growth and dividends. Together, those will deliver around 8 percent a year. That is all you can reasonably expect over the long haul.

QUITTING THE CASINO

After wallowing in 18.2 percent annual returns through the 1990s, collecting just 8 percent a year over the next decade might seem pathetically small. Faced with such slim pickings, many investors will no doubt pursue the beat-the-market fantasy with renewed vigor. But by now, I hope I have convinced you of the foolishness of such a strategy.

So what is the alternative? Instead of aiming for market-beating returns, I would look to capture as much of the market's return as possible by keeping trading costs, fund-management fees, and taxes to a bare minimum.

It is the same argument I made at the end of the previous chapter about diversification. You don't know which will perform better: an undiversified portfolio or a better-diversified alternative. But if you diversify, you will definitely reduce risk. Similarly, no matter how much you trade or what you pay in fund-management fees, you don't know what sort of precost returns you will earn. But if you hold down those costs, you can at least be sure of keeping more of whatever you make. Costs and risk can be controlled. Performance is in the hands of the gods.

What is the best way of capturing as much of the market's return as possible? That would be index funds. Readers of my *Wall Street Journal* columns know to the point of tedium that I am a huge, huge, huge fan of index funds. They are the investor's best friend and Wall Street's worst nightmare.

Index funds simply buy the stocks that make up a market index, in an effort to replicate the index's performance. Usually, they fall slightly short of that goal, because of the costs they incur. If an index fund charges 0.2 percent of assets a year, it will tend to lag behind its target index by that percentage. For instance, if stocks gain 8 percent a year, a low-cost index fund might return 7.8 percent.

This may sound rather uninspiring. But in truth, index funds are a brilliant answer to an otherwise-unsolvable problem. If you try to beat the market, you will almost certainly fail, because of the hefty costs involved. That is why you see actively managed funds lagging behind the market by 1.5 percentage points a year. Index funds take this problem and turn it on its head. Instead of trying to pick better stocks, they aim to incur lower costs. By looking to match the market's performance while charging modest expenses, index funds ensure that they will outperform most other investors, who are weighed down by far higher costs.

All this begs a question: If index funds are such a wonderful investment, why aren't they more popular? Part of the problem is that, while index funds look great over time, they never look that smart in any particular year. An index fund might outpace, say, 55 or 60 percent of competing funds each year. Meanwhile, there are plenty of stock jockeys who are posting far more impressive gains and outperforming 80 or 90 percent of their competitors. With returns like that on offer, why bother with index funds?

Yes, there will always be stock jockeys at the top of the performance charts. The problem is, it is never the same jockey. The highfliers come and go. Meanwhile, index funds plod along, beating 55 or 60 percent of funds year after year. If a fund does that consistently, it will soon rank among the fund industry's top performers. Investing is about getting the small things right. If you save diligently, control risk, hold down costs, trim taxes, and buy index funds, the benefits will be negligible in any given year. But over time, those virtues compound and your small portfolio will snowball into sub-stantial wealth.

In many parts of Wall Street, index funds are pro-foundly unpopular and it is easy to understand why. In-dex funds are a direct challenge to the whole foolish beat-the-market fantasy. Every time an investor gives up trying to beat the market and buys index funds instead, Wall Street becomes a little less profitable. The Street isn't going to get rich off index funds charging 0.2 per-cent a year. The year-end bonuses are a lot fatter when investors trade like crazy and stuff their savings into ac-tively managed funds.

But as an investor, you should consider Wall Street's scorn for index funds to be a glowing endorsement. If it is bad for the Street, there is a decent chance that it is good for you. As Berkshire Hathaway Chairman Warren Buffett wrote in the company's 1996 annual report, "Most investors, both institutional and individual, will find that the best way to own common stocks is through an index fund that charges minimal fees. Those follow-ing this path are sure to beat the net results (after fees and expenses) delivered by the great majority of invest-ment professionals."

By indexing, you don't just ensure that you will do better than most other investors. You will also enjoy the advantage of "relative certainty." In any given year, you don't know how the stock market will perform. But whatever the market delivers, that is what your index funds will get. By contrast, if you pick individual stocks or buy actively managed funds, you can't be sure how you will fare relative to the market and there is a decent chance that your results could be substantially worse.

Indexing is also a highly tax-efficient strategy. If the

performance of index funds looks good before taxes, their results are pretty much unbeatable once you figure in Uncle Sam's cut. Many actively managed stock funds pay scant attention to taxes and they often end up making big capital-gains distributions each year. That is bad news for taxable shareholders who own these funds. If you hold a fund in a taxable account, you have to pay taxes on any distributions the fund makes, even if you reinvest the money in additional fund shares.

By contrast, the annual distributions from stock-index funds are typically fairly modest. True, index funds that own real-estate investment trusts will make big income distributions each year, and you can get unpleasantly large capital-gains distributions from more specialized stock-index funds, such as those focusing on value stocks or small stocks.

Still, these distributions will usually be smaller than those from comparable actively managed funds. Because index funds don't actively manage their portfolios, they tend to realize capital gains only when one of the stocks in the index is acquired or when a company leaves the index. I believe that index funds are a great investment, whether you are investing through a taxable account or a tax-sheltered retirement account. But the case for index funds is especially compelling if you are investing through a taxable account.

TAKING IN THE WORLD

When you put together your mix of stock-index funds, you should build a global portfolio, one that encompasses large, small, and foreign stocks. Many people are reluctant to venture beyond blue-chip U.S. stocks. That reluctance was bolstered by performance in the 1990s. Then, larger U.S. stocks easily outpaced small companies and foreign markets.

But if you take a longer view, the case for building a globally diversified mix looks much stronger. Consider the relative performance of large, small, and foreign stocks in the 1970s, the 1980s, and the 1990s. Among those three market sectors, large U.S. stocks were the winner in the 1990s. But in the 1980s, larger stocks ranked second and, in the 1970s, they were third.

Similarly, small stocks ranked first in the 1970s, third in the 1980s, and second in the 1990s, while foreign markets ranked second in the 1970s, first in the 1980s, and third in the 1990s. In other words, over this 30-year stretch, all three sectors had periods when they were the top performer and all three had spells when they were the global market's cellar dweller.

As always, the temptation is to try to pick the winning sector, ride it for a while, and then hop to the next hot sector. But regrettably, there is no surefire way of doing that. Instead, you are better off holding all three sectors. There are two reasons.

First, you can reduce risk by diversifying globally. If you are heavily invested in large U.S. stocks, adding foreign stocks is one of the best ways of lowering your stock portfolio's risk level. This may seem counterintuitive. We tend to view familiar investments, such as blue-chip stocks, local companies, and our employer's shares, as conservative, while seeing foreign stocks—especially those in emerging markets—as unfamiliar and hence risky.

Nonetheless, if you want a stock-market sector that will do well when blue-chip U.S. stocks are posting lackluster results, adding foreign shares is often your best bet. Part of this diversification comes from currency. When the U.S. market is suffering, the dollar may also tumble, bolstering the value of foreign stocks. That happened in 2002, helping to trim the losses for U.S. holders of foreign stocks. Want to make sure that you get the full benefit of foreign diversification? Stick with foreign-stock funds, such as index funds, that don't hedge their currency exposure.

Second, over the long haul, you probably won't pay much, if any, price in performance for holding a globally diversified stock portfolio. Over the 30 years through December 2001, large stocks returned 12.2 percent a year, small stocks climbed 14.9 percent, and foreign markets gained 11.2 percent. In fact, holding all three sectors can actually lead to results that are better than a weighted average of those three numbers might suggest. It all has to do with rebalancing.

What's rebalancing? It is a simple strategy that turns diversification from a risk-reduction technique into a strategy that can both reduce risk and also bolster returns. The idea is to set target portfolio percentages for your different holdings. You might, for instance, earmark 50 percent of your stock portfolio for large-company stocks, 25 percent for small stocks, and 25 percent for foreign markets.

Thereafter, you occasionally rebalance, to bring your portfolio back into line with these target percentages. That helps to reduce risk further, by ensuring that your portfolio doesn't get overweighted in any one sector. But it also has a pleasant side effect. Assuming that all three sectors post similar long-run returns, this rebalancing will boost performance, because it forces you to lighten up on hot investments that are likely to cool and compels you to add to those investments that are beaten down and should rebound.

And that, indeed, is what would have happened over the past 30 years. If you simply bought and held a mix of 50 percent large stocks, 25 percent small stocks, and 25 percent foreign markets over the 30 years through December 2001, you would have earned 12.9 percent a year. But if you rebalanced back to your target percentages every year, you would have garnered 13.2 percent. Earning an extra 0.3 percent a year may not seem like much. But over 30 years, that would mean big bucks. If you invested $10,000 at 12.9 percent for 30 years, you would amass a little under $381,000. But the same $10,000 at 13.2 percent would grow to almost $412,500, giving you an extra $31,500.

As alluring as rebalancing is, keep a few caveats in mind. For starters, rebalancing is best done with mutual funds, preferably index funds, where you can be confident of earning whatever the market sector delivers. You wouldn't want to try this strategy with individual stocks or high-risk stock funds, because there is a chance that these investments will go down and never come back.

More critically, if you are not careful, rebalancing can mean massive tax bills. You may be able to rebalance by directing fresh savings to underweighted areas. That won't cause any messy tax bills. But to keep your portfolio in balance, you will probably also need to do some selling. If you do that selling in your taxable account, you will likely boost your tax bill and possibly turn your 1040 into an accounting quagmire.

For that reason, rebalancing is best done in a retirement account, where your money grows tax-deferred until it is withdrawn. You can get this tax-deferred growth from a bewildering array of accounts, including 401(k) plans, 403(b) plans, Keogh plans, individual retirement accounts, Roth IRAs, and variable annuities.

What market sectors should you target and how much should you invest in each? Within reason, it doesn't much matter. You hear experts debate endlessly over whether you should allocate 15, 20, or 30 percent of a stock portfolio to foreign stocks. But the key isn't the exact percentage. Over 30 years, all parts of the global stock market should generate roughly comparable returns.

Rather, the key is that you stick with whatever percentages you adopt. If you allocate a lot of your portfolio to a sector that you are not really comfortable owning, you might balk at buying more when it comes time to rebalance. My advice: Include a little bit of everything, but don't adopt target percentages that are higher than you can stomach.

Given that all parts of the global stock market will likely generate fairly similar returns over the next 30 years, you might be inclined to stick exclusively with blue-chip U.S. stocks. But that would mean giving up the risk reduction that comes with diversification and losing the performance bonus that comes from rebalancing.

In addition, your time horizon may turn out to be far shorter than 30 years. What if you suddenly need cash and your need for cash coincides with a long dry spell for blue-chip stocks? If you own only these stocks, you will be sunk. But if you own a globally diversified portfolio, you can raise cash by selling those sectors that have lately performed best, while leaving your blue-chip stocks to bounce back.

Ideally, you want to build your global portfolio with index funds. But that still leaves lots of choices. You could go for supreme simplicity, putting, say, 30 percent in a foreign-stock index fund and 70 percent in a Wilshire 5000–index fund. The Wilshire 5000 includes all regularly traded U.S. stocks, so a Wilshire 5000 fund will give you exposure to both large and small U.S. shares.

But you could get fancier, buying more specialized index funds instead. For instance, you might divide up your foreign exposure, putting $5 in an index fund that mimics developed foreign markets for every $1 you invest in a fund that tracks emerging markets. Similarly, you might pass on a Wilshire 5000 fund and instead split your U.S. exposure, stashing maybe $7 in an S&P 500–index fund for every $3 you invest in an index fund that mimics smaller stocks.

You could go even further, buying four U.S. stock-index funds, a large-company value fund, a large-company growth fund, a small-company value fund, and a small-company growth fund. Growth funds buy richly valued stocks that hold out the promise of fast earnings growth; value funds own stocks that appear cheap compared with assets or current earnings. Put all these funds together and you could end up with a stock-index portfolio that has, say, 25 percent in a large-company value fund, 25 percent in a large-company growth fund, 10 percent in a small-company value fund, 10 percent in a small-company growth fund, 25 percent in a developed—

foreign-markets fund, and 5 percent in an emerging-markets fund.

These more specialized funds will be less tax-efficient than broader-based funds, because gains will be triggered as stocks migrate from one index to the next. Still, if you are investing through a retirement account, it may be worth building your portfolio using these more specialized funds. Why? These more specialized funds will perform more erratically, thus offering a greater chance to enhance returns through rebalancing.

Slicing and dicing the world with index funds, however, may also prove more nerve-racking. Depending on the percentages you adopt, your overall portfolio's short-term performance may stray significantly from the broad market's results. Moreover, you may find yourself fretting over each fund's performance. Their erratic performances may mean that there is more opportunity to rebalance. But you also have to live with those results. In a portfolio of specialized index funds, you will always have one or two funds that are getting knocked around. Don't kid yourself. All that volatility can be difficult to stomach.

WINDOW SHOPPING ON WALL STREET

If you want to buy index funds, there is a slew of firms that offer at least one or two low-cost index funds, including Houston's Bridgeway Funds, New York's TIAA–CREF, and San Antonio's USAA Investment Management. But these firms don't offer all the funds you need to build a well-diversified index-fund portfolio. For that, you might turn to New York's Dreyfus Corp., Boston's Fidelity Investments, Baltimore's T. Rowe Price Associates, or San Francisco's Charles Schwab Corp. All offer index funds that track large U.S. stocks, small U.S. stocks, and foreign markets.

What if you want access to the full panoply of index funds, including more specialized index funds? There are only three choices: San Francisco's Barclays Global Investors; Dimensional Fund Advisors in Santa Monica, California; and Vanguard Group in Malvern, Pennsylvania.

For most investors, Vanguard will be the place to go. Once you decide which indexes you want to track, all that remains is to find mutual funds that levy minimal annual expenses and that don't charge a sales commis-

---

OPERATORS ARE STANDING BY

Barclays Global Investors	1-800-474-2737
Bridgeway Funds	1-800-661-3550
Dimensional Fund Advisors	1-310-395-8005
Dreyfus Corp.	1-800-373-9387
Fidelity Investments	1-800-343-3548
T. Rowe Price Associates	1-800-638-5660
Charles Schwab Corp.	1-800-435-4000
TIAA–CREF	1-800-223-1200
USAA Investment Management	1-800-382-8722
Vanguard Group	1-800-662-7447

sion, often referred to as a "load." On that score, Vanguard is usually the lowest-cost option. The firm offers a huge array of no-load index funds, most of which have a $3,000 investment minimum.

Meanwhile, Barclays' iShares index funds aren't regular mutual funds. Instead, the firm manages a series of exchange-traded index funds, often known as ETFs. These ETFs trade on the stock market, just like any other stock. There are other firms that offer ETFs too, but Barclays has by far the broadest array of funds. Its iShares have annual expenses that are sometimes lower than the cost on comparable Vanguard index-mutual funds. The problem is that when you trade an ETF, you incur brokerage commissions and get nicked by the bid–ask spread. Those costs aren't a big deal if you have a large chunk of money to invest. But if you are a smaller investor or you plan to add regularly to your account, you will be better off with Vanguard's mutual funds.

What about Dimensional Fund Advisors (DFA)? The firm doesn't accept money from small investors. Instead, to invest in DFA's funds, you have to go through an investment adviser registered with DFA. That, of course, raises a key question: Do you need an investment adviser? I believe that most folks are smart enough and disciplined enough to invest without professional help.

But I also realize that there are plenty of people who don't have the emotional fortitude to invest on their own or who don't want the burden of managing their own money. For these investors, a good low-cost adviser may be a great idea. But you will immediately run into two problems: First, how do you figure out if an adviser is any good? And, second, how do you make sure that the costs involved aren't so onerous that they obliterate any chance of earning decent returns?

These are thorny issues. There is no single qualification that will ensure that you are getting a good adviser. There is no magic question that, depending on how the adviser answers, will tell you whether you have a bad apple or a good pick. In selecting an adviser, the profoundly ignorant are, I regret, sheep to the slaughter. You have to know at least a little about investing or you won't be able to tell whether a potential adviser is well informed or determined to mislead.

My recommendation: Before hiring an adviser, spend a good amount of time talking with him or her. What should you listen for? Here are some of the warning signs:

- Avoid advisers who pay scant attention to your goals. If a broker or financial planner doesn't know why you are investing, there is no way that you will get an intelligent investment recommendation.

- Avoid advisers who promise double-digit annual returns. That sort of gain can never be guaranteed.

- Avoid advisers who profess to know safe ways to earn high returns. You can't earn high returns without taking high risk.

- Avoid advisers who boast of market-beating performance. After costs, very few investors manage to beat the market.

■ Avoid advisers who suggest that you will have to trade a lot. That trading will likely wreak havoc with your returns, while greatly enriching the adviser.

■ Avoid advisers who focus almost exclusively on the products you will have to buy. In all likelihood, the products involved will yield fat commissions to the adviser and heartache to unsuspecting investors.

■ Avoid advisers who insist that you need cash-value life insurance. This is one of Wall Street's most over-sold investment products, combining costly life-insurance coverage with mediocre investment performance.

■ Avoid advisers who push you to act quickly. If you are investing for goals that are 20 or 30 years away, why would you need to make a snap decision?

As you hunt for an adviser, you clearly want someone who is experienced. But if you are approaching retirement, you also want somebody who is either younger than you or who works closely with a team of other advisers. Why? Once you are retired, you need an adviser who is still working, so that he or she can help you with some of the tough decisions you will face in your seventies and eighties.

When interviewing an adviser, get some sense of what investment strategy the adviser will recommend and what costs will be involved. I would not sign on with any adviser who wants to be compensated with commissions. When advisers charge commissions, it means they get compensated only when you buy or sell. That creates a terrible conflict of interest. In extreme cases, advisers will push clients to trade excessively, resulting in fat commissions for the adviser and terrible returns for the investor.

On the other hand, if an adviser talks about the sort of strategies recommended in this book and uses DFA, iShares, or Vanguard funds, you can breathe a little easier. With those funds, you should be able to build a portfolio that costs 0.4 percent a year or less. But remember, the adviser's fee will be layered on top of that.

How much will that fee be? Advisers who recommend index funds usually don't get compensated through commissions. Instead, they charge a percentage of assets. These days, the standard fee is 1 percent. Add that to the 0.4 percent in fund expenses and you are losing 1.4 percent a year, which strikes me as a little steep. If I were using an adviser, I would want the combined cost of the adviser and the recommended funds to come in at 1 percent a year or less.

These lower-cost advisers are difficult to find, but they are out there. Don't bother asking your insurance agent, who will try to get you to buy costly products such as cash-value life insurance, and don't go looking at the big brokerage firms, where you will likely end up with a high-cost investment strategy pushed by a commission-hungry broker.

So where can you find these low-cost advisers? Ask your friends. Contact the National Association of Personal Financial Advisors and get a list of financial planners in your area. Search the Web. You will discover that there are outfits such as Portfolio Solutions in Troy, Michigan, which will manage money for as little as 0.25

percent a year. Vanguard Group also offers an investment-advisory service, for which it charges 0.65 percent annually. To find Web addresses for these and other organizations mentioned here, check out the appendix at the back of this book.

While paying a percentage of assets is far better than paying commissions, it is not ideal. Why not? Advisers who charge a percentage of assets have an incentive to keep as much of your money under their management as possible. But that may not always be in your best interest. It could be that you should use part of your portfolio to pay down your mortgage, buy an immediate-fixed annuity, or open 529 college-savings plans for your children or grandchildren. All of these can be smart investments. But unethical advisers won't mention these possibilities, because it will reduce the money they manage and hence reduce their fees.

Given this potential conflict of interest, don't rule out other payment arrangements. Some firms now levy an annual retainer, which can turn out to be far cheaper. For instance, Evanson Asset Management in Monterey, California, charges a retainer that might run $2,000 a year.

There is also a burgeoning number of advisers who will give advice for an hourly fee, typically around $150 an hour. Many of these advisers are members of the Garrett Planning Network in Shawnee, Kansas. If you want to manage your own money, but would occasionally like a financial checkup or a second opinion, these hourly advisers can be an excellent choice. These advisers may also be your best option if you have a relatively small portfolio and thus you don't meet the $400,000 or $500,000 account minimum demanded by many full-time investment advisers.

4 BANKING ON BONDS

It's enough to give you whiplash.

In the heady days of early 2000, stocks were hailed as a one-way ticket to wealth, while bonds were derided as the choice of wimps. Three years later, bonds are beloved for their steady gains, while stocks are dismissed as dead money.

This about-face is mildly amusing. But it is also a prescription for investment mediocrity. Chasing performance got investors into trouble in the late 1990s, as they loaded up on technology stocks just ahead of the crash. Yet, here we are, chasing performance all over again. Even as stocks suffered painful losses in 2000, 2001, and 2002, bonds scored healthy gains. Those gains haven't gone unnoticed by investors, who have been dumping stocks and buying bonds instead. But where is the logic in buying what has already performed well? It may be comforting to own an investment that has lately posted big gains. But you can't eat past performance. If you buy today, what counts is the future.

Will today's love affair with bonds end badly? The answer, I believe, depends on which bonds you buy. In 2002, as the search for safety became more frantic, investors poured money into Treasury bonds. That buying frenzy drove the yield on the benchmark 10-year Treasury note below 4 percent, the lowest level in four decades.

At such a miserably low yield, Treasuries are unlikely to give investors much to smile about, especially once inflation and taxes are figured in. After all, if you collect 4 percent in interest and lose 27 percent of that sum to federal income taxes, you will be left with just under 3 percent. Subtract two or three percentage points for inflation and your gain is largely or entirely wiped out.

Moreover, there is a risk that interest rates will climb as inflation heats up and economic growth accelerates. As every novice investor eventually discovers, interest rates and bond prices move in opposite directions. If interest rates climb, bond prices will tumble, leaving Treasury investors with painful losses. Even after adding back the interest they collect, these folks may find themselves underwater in any given year. It has happened before. For instance, between 1977 and 1980, long-term government bonds suffered four consecutive calendar-year losses.

While the outlook for traditional Treasury bonds doesn't seem great, other bonds look like a decent bet for the next 10 years. What sort of bonds should you buy? Consider purchasing a mix of inflation-indexed Treasury bonds, high-quality corporate bonds, and high-yield junk bonds. A diversified portfolio of those bonds probably won't keep up with stocks. But the bonds may not be too far behind.

To understand why, recall Chapter 3's analysis of stock returns. If earnings per share grow 6 percent a year and dividends kick in another 2 percent, we are looking at a long-run return on the Standard & Poor's 500-stock index of maybe 8 percent a year. Small U.S. stocks and foreign shares may do somewhat better.

Nonetheless, once you figure in investment costs, you are unlikely to do much better than 8 percent annually.

How will bonds stack up against that 8 percent? Traditionally, stock investors have turned to bonds to get portfolio protection, because the bonds can help cushion any stock-market decline. But what about performance? Historically, bonds have been the big loser, trailing stocks by some five percentage points a year over the past 75 years.

You would expect some underperformance. When you buy a stock, you become part owner of the corporation, thereby getting a chance to participate in the company's growth. But when you purchase bonds, you are merely lending money, in return for which you collect interest. As such, there is a limit to the gains you can enjoy. Still, in the years ahead, I suspect investors will buy bonds not only for portfolio protection, but also for their raw results. The bond market is likely to underperform stocks by far less than five percentage points a year. Indeed, some bonds may deliver returns that rival those on stocks.

For high-quality bonds, the best guide to their probable return is their current yield. If you purchase a basket of high-quality bonds that yield 5 percent, your return over the next decade probably won't stray too far from that 5 percent. Sure, your annual total return might be slightly higher or lower, depending on what happens to bond prices. But the biggest determinant of your performance is going to be that starting yield.

Which brings us to a key question: Where can you find decent yields? Both high-quality and high-yield corporate bonds look attractive. But don't just scan the bond market. Also take a close look at your debts. Puzzled? Let me explain.

TAKING CREDIT

When you buy bonds, you lend money. Sometimes, you might be lending to the federal government by buying Treasury bonds. Sometimes, you are helping out big corporations by purchasing corporate bonds. Sometimes, your money goes to homeowners, whose mortgages are bundled together into mortgage-backed bonds. Sometimes, you are lending money to the local town or city government by investing in its municipal bonds.

But in the end, many of us aren't big lenders of money. Instead, we are big borrowers. Think about all the debts you have. You might have a balance outstanding on your credit cards. You probably have a mortgage. Maybe you also have car loans and student loans. Instead of buying bonds and earning interest, many of us find ourselves going into debt and paying interest.

Try this exercise. First, total up all your debts. Next, compare this sum to the amount you have in bonds and other interest-earning investments, such as savings accounts and certificates of deposit. Unless you are a retiree or close to retirement age, you probably owe a lot more than you are owed. In effect, you have a negative position in bonds. Want to boost the net amount you have in bonds? Instead of purchasing more bonds, you may find that it makes more sense to slash your debts.

Sad to say, but you and I are considered to be somewhat shady characters, especially when compared to the U.S. government and major corporations. Those guys can borrow money at rock-bottom interest rates. But when you and I borrow money, we are often dunned for steep interest charges. That is certainly true of credit-card debt. If you have any sort of card debt, paying off that balance is one of the smartest investments you can make. Suppose you have credit-card debt that costs you 17 percent a year. If you pay off that debt, you will avoid that 17 percent annual cost.

That is a pretty handsome return on your investment. You are unlikely to notch 17 percent by buying stocks or bonds. In fact, probably the only investment that is sure to earn you a higher return is investing in a 401(k) plan with a company match. If the company is matching your contributions dollar for dollar, your first-year return is effectively 100 percent, even if you don't clock any investment gains. Maxed out on your 401(k) contributions and still have more money to invest? Forget stocks and bonds. Any additional spare dollars should go toward paying off your credit cards and other high-interest debt.

As an added bonus, this debt reduction will buy you some valuable financial flexibility. Think about your fixed monthly costs. Between the money you fork over for cell phones, minimum credit-card payments, Internet access, car loans, utility bills, cable television, and your mortgage, probably a hefty portion of your monthly income is already spoken for. What if you lose your job or get hit with major medical expenses? That is always going to be unpleasant. But it will be a lot less unpleasant if your monthly financial obligations are small.

NO PLACE LIKE HOME

With any luck, you won't have too much credit-card debt. You may, however, have a ton of mortgage debt. Should you look to pay off your home loan early? Mortgage debt isn't nearly as costly as credit-card debt. The interest rates are far lower and, unlike credit-card debt, you may be able to deduct your mortgage interest on Schedule A of your federal tax return. Even so, it frequently makes sense to make extra-principal payments with a view to paying off your mortgage more quickly.

That contention, however, often generates a whirl-wind of confusion. What confuses folks? Some people look at the mortgage company as the joint owner of their house and view paying down their mortgage as somehow increasing their investment in real estate. But in reality, you don't own the house jointly with the mortgage company. Instead, you own the whole thing. The mortgage company simply lent you money. When you pay down your mortgage, what you are doing is reducing that debt and thereby avoiding future interest payments.

Which brings us to a second source of confusion. A lot of people figure that the interest they pay is pretty much a freebie, because they get to deduct it on their tax return. But this deduction isn't as valuable as many people imagine.

Suppose you are in the 27 percent federal income-tax bracket. This 27 percent isn't the average tax rate applied to your income. Rather, it is the tax rate applied to the last few dollars of income you earn each year. You can figure out your marginal tax rate when filling out your annual Form 1040 for the Internal Revenue Service.

Just look at the formula used to calculate how much you owe in taxes. The percentage included in the tax formula indicates your marginal tax rate.

Now, suppose you incur $1,000 of tax-deductible mortgage interest. If you are in the 27 percent tax bracket, you will save $270 in taxes, which means your out-of-pocket cost is still $730. Your $1,000 of interest is only tax-deductible if you itemize your deductions using Schedule A. But most people don't itemize, which means the $1,000 of interest is costing them the full $1,000. Moreover, even if you do file Schedule A, you may see the value of your itemized deduction curtailed if your income is too high.

Still, let us assume that you can deduct all your mortgage interest and that you just borrowed $200,000 through a 30-year fixed-rate mortgage costing 6.5 percent. Your monthly mortgage payment would be $1,264. Now, suppose you rounded that sum up to $1,400, by adding $136 to each monthly payment. If you did that, your required monthly payment wouldn't go down. But you would still reap a huge reward. Thanks to the extra $136 a month, you would pay off your 30-year mortgage in just 23 years, thereby saving yourself almost $70,000 in interest.

Impressed? Even though the savings can be enormous, that doesn't mean paying down your mortgage is always your best bet. It all depends on the alternatives. If your mortgage rate is 6.5 percent and you are in the 27 percent income-tax bracket, the loan's after-tax cost is 4.75 percent. You ought to be able to earn more than that each year by buying stocks or bonds through an individual retirement account, a 401(k) plan, or some other tax-sheltered retirement account. You should also earn somewhat more than that 4.75 percent by buying stocks in a taxable account.

But what if you want to buy bonds in your taxable account? It is time to compare yields. A corporate bond yielding 6 percent might seem more compelling than paying down your mortgage, with its 4.75 percent after-tax cost. Remember, however, that if you hold that 6 percent bond in a taxable account, you will have to pay tax each year on the interest you collect. After losing 27 percent to taxes, you will be left with 4.38 percent. Thus, paying down your mortgage will probably be the smarter bet.

As you weigh whether to pay down your mortgage, there are other factors to consider. If you pay off your mortgage more quickly, that can buy you a substantial amount of financial freedom, making it easier to retire or to put your kids through college. On the other hand, if you want easy access to your money, it may make sense to shovel extra cash into stock and bond funds held in your taxable account. True, you can always tap into your home's value using a home-equity loan or line of credit. But often it is a lot easier and cheaper to sell a few mutual-fund shares.

COMING UP SHORT

You have paid off your high-cost debt. Now, you are looking to purchase bonds. But what should you buy? Most investors should steer clear of individual bonds and instead plunk for bond funds. As with stocks, it is all about diversification. Even seemingly robust corporations go bankrupt and holders of their bonds often don't recoup all of their money, so you need the protection that comes from spreading your money across a slew of different issues.

In addition, the bond market can be a rough place for individual investors. The market is dominated by professional money managers with millions, and sometimes billions, to invest. Have $5,000 or $10,000 to invest in an individual bond? You won't get a whole lot of respect. You will likely pay too much when you buy individual bonds and get too little when you sell. By contrast, if you buy a mutual fund, you pool your money with other small investors, thus turning yourself into an institutional investor and putting yourself on par with other bond-market heavyweights.

For your first bond fund, I would opt for a short-term bond fund with low annual expenses and a hefty stake in corporate bonds. Many of the fund companies mentioned at the end of the previous chapter, including Fidelity, T. Rowe Price, Schwab, TIAA–CREF, USAA, and Vanguard, offer short-term bond funds that don't levy a sales commission. These funds typically own a mix of corporate and government bonds with maybe two or three years to maturity.

As you will discover, the yields on short-term corporate-bond funds are decent, but not great. You will almost certainly do better by buying stocks or paying down your mortgage. Nonetheless, these funds will make a useful addition to your portfolio. Have cash languishing in a savings account or a money-market fund? By swapping the money into a short-term corporate-bond fund, you can bolster the interest you earn, without taking on a whole lot more risk.

But there is some risk. Unlike a savings account, a short-term corporate-bond fund can lose money. All bonds and bond funds get whacked when interest rates climb, which means you could get a disappointingly low price if you suddenly need to sell. The losses, however, will be relatively modest for short-term bond funds, and certainly a lot smaller than the hit to funds that hold bonds with longer to maturity.

In fact, once you figure in the interest you collect, you are unlikely to have a calendar-year loss with a short-term corporate-bond fund, even if interest rates climb sharply. For proof, consider Vanguard Short-Term Corporate Fund. Launched in 1982, the fund has failed to make money in only one calendar year, and that was a tiny 0.08 percent loss in 1994. While short-term bonds are far less risky than longer-term issues, you don't sacrifice a lot of yield by favoring the lower-risk option. Often, you can pick up most of the yield of longer-term bonds by buying comparable-quality issues with just three or five years to maturity.

Want to collect a little more interest than that offered by short-term corporate bonds? If you are tempted to stretch for yield by buying intermediate-term bonds, I would consider purchasing a low-cost bond-index fund. These funds, like their stock-index–fund cousins, seek to track the performance of a designated market average, while keeping costs to a minimum. That strategy has proved to be a winner, with bond-index funds outperforming most competing funds.

Dreyfus, T. Rowe Price, Schwab, and Vanguard offer bond-index funds that track the total bond market, which means that on average these funds hold intermediate-term bonds, those with around eight years to maturity. One caveat: Bond-index funds invest in a broad mix of government and corporate bonds. As a result, these funds could struggle if investors become less antsy and start lightening up on government bonds, causing those bonds to fall in price.

Whatever bond funds you buy, keep your costs to a minimum. Favor no-load funds, which don't charge any sort of sales commission, over broker-sold load funds. Also, pick funds with low annual expenses. Once again, it is a matter of getting the little things right and then reaping your reward over time. In any given year, favoring low-cost bond funds won't greatly improve your portfolio's performance. But with time, the virtues of low cost shine through and the benefits are huge.

Indeed, differences in annual expenses are the biggest determinant of differences in bond-fund performance. In a study published in the Winter 1999 *Journal of Investing,* Baylor University investments professor William Reichenstein analyzed bond funds in seven categories, looking at their performance over the five years through year-end 1998. For each category, he divided the funds into three groups, based on their annual expenses. Result? In each of the seven categories, the low-cost group of funds had the best five-year total returns, while the high-cost funds had the poorest performance.

To find out whether a fund levies a sales commission and how much it charges in annual expenses, call the fund involved and talk to one of the telephone representatives or ask the representative to send you a prospectus. Alternatively, look up the fund at the Web site offered by Chicago fund researchers Morningstar Inc. (www.morningstar.com).

I would stick with no-load short-term bond funds

TAXING MATTERS

Should you hold stocks in your retirement account and bonds in your taxable account, or vice versa? Among financial experts, this is the subject of an ongoing, and often tedious, debate. But forget the debate. The right advice hinges on how you manage your money.

My recommendation: Aim to keep your bond funds in your 401(k), 403(b), and other retirement accounts, while holding your stock-index funds in your taxable account. Why? Most of the gain from bonds takes the form of interest, which is immediately taxable as ordinary income. By holding your bond funds in retirement accounts, you defer those income taxes until you retire and start making retirement-account withdrawals.

By contrast, with a stock-index fund, most of your gain will come from share-price appreciation. That appreciation will usually be taxed at the lower capital-gains rate. For instance, if you are in the 27 percent or higher income-tax bracket, your capital gains will be taxed at 20 percent if you hold investments for over a year and possibly just 18 percent if you hang on for five years. The 18 percent rate applies starting in 2006.

Moreover, you don't have to pay those capital-gains taxes until your gains are realized. Because index funds don't actively trade their portfolios, your funds shouldn't realize a lot of capital gains each year. You, of course, could trigger capital gains by selling fund shares. But as long as you stick with them, your stock-index funds should give you tax-deferral, just like a retirement account. In early 2003, Congress was discussing a new law that would make dividends partially or entirely tax-free. If that comes to pass, holding stocks in your taxable account would make even more sense.

In all this, I am assuming that you follow the advice in Chapter 3, buying stock-index funds and investing for the long haul. What if you plan to buy actively managed funds or you figure you will trade in and out of your stock funds? In that case, ignore what I just said. You should do the precise opposite, holding your stock funds in your retirement account. That way, you will limit some of the damage done by your trading and by your funds' trading, because you will defer taxes on any realized stock-market gains.

Because you are now using your retirement account to hold stocks, you may have to keep your bonds in your taxable account. Unfortunately, those bonds will now be immediately taxable. As a result, you might want to favor municipal bonds, assuming that your tax bracket is 27 percent or higher. Munis kick off interest that is exempt from federal taxes. If you own bonds from your own state, that interest should also be exempt from state and possibly local taxes. But in return for these tax-free gains, you collect a lower yield than you would receive from taxable bonds.

In other words, your insistence on trading too much and purchasing actively managed funds will almost certainly hurt your portfolio's performance. It is not just that your actively managed stock funds are likely to lag behind the market average. In addition, your bond performance will suffer, because you are buying lower-yielding municipals in your taxable account, rather than the higher-yielding taxable bonds that you could have held in your retirement account.

In divvying up investments between your taxable and retirement accounts, tailor the above advice to your situation. In particular, don't let your mix of taxable and retirement money determine your stock–bond mix.

Suppose you have a generous 401(k) plan that you want to fund to the fullest each year. In that case, you will likely end up buying both bond and stock funds in your retirement account. That is a great situation to be in. If you can hold at least some of your stock funds in your retirement account, that will ease some of the tax hassles that come with rebalancing, as mentioned in Chapter 3.

On the other hand, you may find yourself short on tax-sheltered money. You can always open an individual retirement account, assuming that you have earned income. But maybe you don't have a 401(k) or 403(b) at work, and thus you can't get tax-deferral for all your bonds. That, however, doesn't mean you should skimp on bonds. Instead, consider either buying a tax-deferred fixed annuity or purchasing bonds through a low-cost tax-deferred variable annuity. What about your stock-index funds? You can keep those in your taxable account.

with annual expenses of 0.5 percent a year or less. Schwab, TIAA–CREF, and Vanguard all have funds that meet these criteria. Only Vanguard's fund is a pure corporate-bond fund; the others include some government bonds. As you think about costs, also pay attention to the biggest investment cost of all, taxes. For more on that, see the accompanying box, Taxing Matters.

DEFENDING PRINCIPAL

For skittish investors, it can be unnerving to own investments that fluctuate in value. Funnily enough, these misgivings can affect us more with bonds than with stocks. We expect stocks to be wild and crazy. But with bonds, we look for stability, so any losses can really sting, even if those losses are relatively modest.

Still, I believe it would be a huge mistake to leave cash languishing in savings accounts, money-market funds, and other low-yield investments. After inflation and taxes, there is a good chance that you will lose money. At a minimum, consider moving this cash into a short-term corporate-bond fund, which will give you a more generous yield. But maybe you are leery of short-term corporate-bond funds, because you don't like the idea of even modest share-price fluctuations. What to do? If you want decent yields without risking principal, consider two alternatives.

First, if you have a 401(k) plan at work, see if it includes a stable-value fund. These funds aim to maintain the value of investors' principal, while generating a healthy yield by investing in high-quality corporate bonds and guaranteed investment contracts issued by insurance companies. A stable-value fund won't make you rich. But you will earn more than you would with a money-market fund, without taking on a whole lot more risk.

Second, if you are investing outside your employer's plan, give some thought to tax-deferred fixed annuities. The term *annuity* covers a ragtag of investments that are issued by insurance companies, often in association with mutual-fund companies. Some annuities are good and some are not so good. How do you distinguish among them? There are four varieties:

■ *Immediate-fixed annuities.* These can be used to generate income in retirement. As you will discover in Chapter 7, I am a fan of immediate-fixed annuities.

■ *Immediate-variable annuities.* These can also be used to generate retirement income. I am far less keen on immediate-variable annuities, which involve greater risk and often outrageously high investment costs.

■ *Tax-deferred variable annuities.* I would avoid almost all tax-deferred variable annuities, which let you save for retirement by choosing from a menu of mutual funds held within the annuity. Most tax-deferred variable annuities are a terrible investment, because the costs involved are so steep. But there are two exceptions: TIAA–CREF and Vanguard. Both have tax-deferred variable annuities with modest expenses.

■ *Tax-deferred fixed annuities.* Like a tax-deferred variable annuity, these are used to accumulate retirement savings. Think of tax-deferred fixed annuities as comparable to buying a bond fund. But there are two key differences: With a tax-deferred fixed annuity, your principal is guaranteed and your interest grows tax-deferred. That tax-deferral may be especially appealing if you don't have a lot of other opportunities to get tax-deferred growth.

As with other tax-deferred accounts, buying a tax-deferred fixed annuity means losing flexibility. You shouldn't invest any money you will need before age 59½. If you withdraw money prior to that, you will probably get hit with tax penalties, in addition to the income taxes owed. But if you can live with that restriction, tax-deferred fixed annuities offer a decent way for conservative investors to garner moderate gains.

Make sure you pick your fixed annuity carefully. Avoid annuities that tout high first-year teaser rates and pay careful attention to the surrender charges involved. Fixed annuities are usually sold through financial advisers. But you can buy them directly.

For instance, Fidelity, Schwab, USAA, and Vanguard all sell stand-alone fixed annuities. But you may prefer to purchase a tax-deferred variable annuity that includes a fixed annuity among its menu of investment options. A number of variable annuities offer that choice, including those managed by Fidelity, T. Rowe Price, TIAA–CREF, and USAA.

Vanguard's variable annuity doesn't include a fixed option. Even so, don't rule out Vanguard's variable annuity. Not only does it have low expenses, but also it offers the chance to invest in many of the tax-inefficient investments mentioned in this book, such as bond-index funds, high-yield junk bonds, and real-estate investment trusts. Because these investments are so tax-inefficient, you wouldn't want to hold them in a regular, taxable account. If you don't have a retirement plan at work and you are looking for other places to get tax-deferred growth for your tax-inefficient investments, Vanguard's variable annuity may be a good choice.

One last caveat: Before purchasing a fixed or variable annuity, check on the financial strength of the insurance company involved. To that end, visit the Web sites offered by some of the credit-rating agencies. You can find their Web addresses in the appendix.

INFLATING YOUR GAINS

If you are a stock-market investor, the two biggest threats are accelerating inflation and slowing economic growth. Both inflation and recession can send stock prices reeling. Your goal is to buy investments that fare well in these two scenarios, thereby lowering your stock portfolio's risk level.

Which investments perform well in a recession? When the economy slows, interest rates tend to fall as inflationary pressures ease, demand for borrowed money falters, and the Federal Reserve cuts short-term interest rates to revive economic growth. In that environment, bonds often sparkle. The biggest gains go to those bonds with the longest time to maturity, because these bonds are most sensitive to interest-rate changes. The problem is, these long-term bonds can get badly roughed up when inflation revives. That is why I favor short-term bonds. But even with short-term bonds, you will get hurt if inflation spikes up and we get an accompanying rise in interest rates.

That means you need another investment in your arsenal, one to combat inflation. Which investments fare well during periods of accelerating inflation? Gold, natural-resource companies, and real estate can all be good hedges against a rapid rise in consumer prices. But if you want protection against inflation, my top choice would be inflation-indexed Treasury bonds.

First introduced in January 1997, these bonds provide a guaranteed yield above inflation. Suppose you buy when the bonds are yielding 2.5 percent and inflation is running at 3 percent a year. In that case, the principal value of your bonds will be stepped up by 3 percent annually, plus you will get an additional bonus, in the form of the 2.5 percent yield. This 2.5 percent is referred to as a real yield, because it represents your gain above inflation. Combine that 2.5 percent real yield with 3 percent inflation and you will have a 5.5 percent annual total return.

For much of their life, inflation-indexed Treasuries offered a yield above inflation of 3 percent or more. But in early 2003, the real yield hovered around 2.5 percent, making the bonds somewhat less compelling. Still, even at these levels, the bonds are a useful addition to your portfolio. They provide great protection against inflation, thus helping to reduce your portfolio's risk. And if stock returns turn out to be lower than my forecasted 8 percent, the returns on inflation-indexed Treasuries could be competitive with those on stocks.

My advice: As a cushion against falling stock prices, consider adding both inflation-indexed Treasury bonds and a short-term corporate-bond fund to your investment mix. That way, your portfolio should fare reasonably well, no matter what the next crisis brings, whether it is slower economic growth or higher inflation.

Dreyfus, Fidelity, T. Rowe Price, TIAA–CREF, and Vanguard Group all offer low-cost bond funds that invest in inflation-indexed Treasury bonds. But in this instance, don't rule out buying individual bonds. Most of the time, it pays to get the diversification that comes with a bond mutual fund. But with Treasury bonds, where there is essentially no credit risk, diversification isn't necessary and it is safe to own individual securities. For those intrigued by Treasuries, you can buy them cheaply and easily through TreasuryDirect, the government program for selling both regular Treasury bonds and inflation-indexed bonds directly to the public without commission. To find out more, visit www.treasurydirect.gov.

Whether you buy a fund or individual inflation-indexed Treasury bonds, consider holding them in a tax-sheltered retirement account. With inflation-indexed

Treasuries, you have to pay federal income taxes each year on both the real yield and the inflation-driven step-up in principal. As a result, these bonds aren't especially tax-efficient and are best held in a retirement account.

What if you are determined to hold inflation-indexed bonds in your taxable account? Check out the government's Series I savings bonds. If you hang onto your savings bonds, you can defer all federal income taxes for up to 30 years. In effect, you get the same sort of tax-deferral that you get with a retirement account. Moreover, you don't have to pay state and local taxes on the interest earned.

But in return for getting these tax benefits, you pay a price in yield. The problem is, the price has lately been a little too steep for my taste. As of early 2003, Series I savings bonds were yielding a paltry 1.6 percentage points a year above inflation. That is not only less than the interest rate on comparable inflation-indexed Treasury bonds, but also it is far below the real yield of 3.6 percent offered by Series I bonds in 2000. The yields on savings bonds are reset May 1 and November 1. I would wait for higher yields before buying. To learn more about savings bonds, including the current yields offered, go to www.savingsbonds.gov.

RUMMAGING THROUGH THE JUNKYARD

While short-term corporate bonds and inflation-indexed bonds probably won't outpace stocks in the decade ahead, I figure that there is a decent chance that you could get stock-like returns from high-yield junk bonds. To be sure, junk bonds aren't for the faint of heart. There is a reason for those high yields. The companies that issue these bonds are considered sufficiently shaky that there is a real risk that they could default on their interest payments.

But with that risk comes the possibility of handsome rewards. We are talking about stock returns of maybe 8 percent a year. Meanwhile, you can buy high-yield junk bonds and get lush double-digit yields. Even with some bond defaults, you could still earn 9 or 10 percent a year, with the possibility of doing somewhat better if junk-bond prices rebound from the depressed levels of early 2003.

Those sorts of returns would have been considered uninspiring during the 1990s bull market. Back then, nobody paid much attention to collecting dividends and interest. Instead, it was all about picking stock-market winners. But if the 1990s were about capital gains, I figure this will be the decade of the dividend and the interest payment. In fact, we have seen this already. Bonds have outperformed stocks. Meanwhile, among stocks, the biggest winners this decade have been dividend-paying companies, while no-yield stocks have suffered the biggest losses.

If low returns persist, high-yield investments will likely continue to sparkle. That would be good news for junk bonds. In 2000, 2001, and 2002, these bonds struggled, as investors worried that the recession would cause a wave of defaults. But as the economy recovers, those worries will ease and high-yield junk bonds should generate decent gains.

Nonetheless, there will still be defaults, so your long-run return is likely to be somewhat less than the yield advertised on the junk-bond mutual fund you buy. Even as your junk fund pays fat dividends, you should expect its shares to gradually lose value, as some of the fund's holdings get into financial trouble and stop paying interest. As a rule of thumb, be prepared to lose about two percentage points a year to defaults. But that will still leave you with a decent return, thanks to the hefty yield from those bonds that continue to pay interest.

Most bond funds are tax-inefficient. But junk-bond funds are the worst, ranking as Uncle Sam's best buddy, so you should buy them only through a retirement account. Fidelity and T. Rowe Price offer junk-bond funds with annual expenses around 0.8 percent, while TIAA–CREF and Vanguard have funds with expenses closer to 0.3 percent. Be warned: These funds vary widely in their risk taking. For instance, Vanguard's offering is extremely tame for a junk-bond fund, while Fidelity's two no-load junk-bond funds may be a better bet for investors who want a pure play on the junk-bond market.

All this talk of sticking bonds in your 401(k) plan or individual retirement account might leave you uneasy. What if you get hit with a financial emergency? In that situation, wouldn't you want to have your more conservative investments in your taxable account, so that you could sell them to raise cash?

There is a crafty way around this dilemma. Suppose you have $10,000 in your taxable account, all of it invested in a stock-index fund. Suddenly, you desperately need that $10,000 to pay for a major home repair. But you are reluctant to sell your stock-index fund, because it is deeply underwater. You do have plenty of money in bonds. But those bonds are in your individual retirement account. That is clearly a problem. You don't want to make a retirement-account withdrawal, because that will trigger both income taxes and, probably, tax penalties.

But there is a way out of this financial conundrum. Cash in your taxable account's stock-index fund. If it really is underwater, that will generate a tax loss. At the same time, within your retirement account, move $10,000 out of bonds and into a stock-index fund. What will all this maneuvering achieve? You will still have the same amount invested in stocks. You won't trigger tax penalties for making an early retirement-account withdrawal. And, best of all, you will have the $10,000 you so urgently need.

5 BETTING ON BRICKS

Ask folks about their house, and you can be confident of two things: One, they will claim that their home is the best investment they ever made. Two, they are totally delusional.

Couples put down $30,000 on a $150,000 house, sell the place 30 years later for over half-a-million dollars, and consider themselves to be financially astute, wonderfully wealthy, and beneficiaries of the great American dream. But in truth, they haven't a clue what they are talking about.

Partly, such claims result from a mix of bad math and financial illusion. But they also, I suspect, reflect the problem with familiarity, mentioned in Chapter 3. We tend to be most comfortable with investments we are most familiar with, such as our employer's stock, savings accounts, certificates of deposit, and shares of local companies and brand-name–product manufacturers. Ditto for real estate. Sure, we never really understood those technology stocks. But houses we understand. After all, we own one of the darn things. It is our biggest investment and we know the place inside and out.

Given all that, maybe it isn't surprising that the stock-market collapse has sent chastened investors scurrying home. Interest in real estate has soared. In fact, property prices have lately been so hot that some pundits have suggested that real estate is in a bubble, comparable to the late 1990s bubble in stocks. I have no opinion on the bubble talk. But this much is clear to me: A lot of people will be sorely disappointed with their foray into real estate.

CAPITAL PUNISHMENT

Take the half-million–dollar home described above. Let us assume that you were the lucky owner. How much did you make on the house? You put down $30,000. Thirty years later, you sold for, say, $515,000, giving you a 9.9 percent annual return. Sound impressive? Unfortunately, that isn't your capital gain. You paid the rest of the $150,000 purchase price through 30 years of mortgage payments.

So if the house cost you $150,000 and you sold for $515,000, how much did you earn? Your gain would be 4.2 percent a year. During that stretch, inflation might have run at 3 percent a year, giving you a return of 1.2 percentage points a year above inflation. That is nothing to write home about. Indeed, you could probably do better with savings bonds and certificates of deposit.

Have a suspicion that I am cooking the numbers? Guess what. I am. I wanted the figures to be realistic. Since 1975, homes have appreciated at 1.2 percentage points a year faster than inflation, according to home-finance corporation Freddie Mac. Freddie Mac's numbers indicate that homes gained 5.8 percent a year over that stretch, while inflation ran at 4.6 percent.

If that gain seems awfully modest, it gets worse. When you bought your $150,000 house, you were likely dinged for a home inspection, title insurance, mortgage-application costs, and legal fees. You might also have paid points to get a lower interest rate on your mortgage. But even without points, your total closing costs could amount to $3,000. Meanwhile, if you sell your home after 30 years, you might pay 6 percent to the selling broker. Figure in those costs and your annual gain on the house would fall to just 3.9 percent, barely above our assumed 3 percent inflation rate.

But, alas, you won't collect even that much. After all, there are also the hefty annual costs associated with owning a house, including homeowner's insurance, property taxes, and home maintenance. Those figures will vary widely across the country. Insurance costs will be higher if you live in an area that is prone to floods, hurricanes, or earthquakes. Property taxes will depend on the cost of local government and how it collects revenue. Meanwhile, home-maintenance costs will vary with the harshness of the climate. But as a rule of thumb, your home-maintenance costs might run to 1 or 2 percent of your home's value each year, though you may get away with a smaller annual hit if you own a recently constructed home.

Subtract all these costs from your home's annual gain and it is clear that your great real-estate investment isn't even close to keeping pace with inflation. Still think that homes deserve to be America's favorite investment? Here comes the knockout blow. We have run the numbers so far and found that our hypothetical home hasn't kept pace with inflation. And yet we haven't even figured in the biggest cost of all, which is the mortgage interest you would have paid.

You put down $30,000 and borrowed the rest of the

$150,000 purchase price. Over the next three decades, the resulting $120,000 loan would have cost you over $153,000 in mortgage interest, assuming you took out a 30-year fixed-rate mortgage with a 6.5 percent interest rate. True, you can probably deduct that mortgage interest on your tax return. But if you are in the 27 percent federal income-tax bracket, your after-tax cost would still amount to almost $112,000.

To be fair, the whole calculation is a little more complicated than I present it here. For instance, to figure out an accurate 30-year rate of return, you would need to take into account the timing of all the various costs associated with home ownership. Similarly, you would need to make adjustments for the likely rise in property taxes, maintenance costs, and insurance over the 30 years.

Still, all this doesn't change the basic point. If you simply compare the $150,000 purchase price with the $515,000 selling price, you might be lulled into thinking that you made $365,000. But in reality, most of this gain would be eaten up by costs.

Fans of real estate respond that the numbers can be far more compelling, thanks to the leverage that results from all the borrowed money. Leverage won't help your returns if you own your home long enough to pay off the mortgage. At that point, the leverage is gone. But if you sell before the mortgage is paid off, leverage can indeed give a surprising boost to your gain. Let us again assume that you bought a $150,000 home, put down $30,000, and borrowed the remaining $120,000. But instead of keeping the house for the full 30 years, you sell seven years later for $210,000.

Your home's value would have climbed from

$150,000 to $210,000, a cumulative increase of 40 percent. But your percentage gain appears to be far larger. When you bought the house, you put down $30,000, which represents your initial home equity. After seven years, your home equity will be at least $90,000, thanks to the $60,000 in appreciation. Result: You have a 200 percent gain.

Or maybe not. Remember, you have the costs of buying and selling, plus ongoing expenses such as insurance, taxes, and maintenance. Between them, those costs would cancel out most of your $60,000 gain. But once again, the real killer is the mortgage. Over the seven years, you would have coughed up $52,000 in interest, while paying off just $11,500 of the $120,000 that you originally borrowed.

This example highlights a key flaw in the whole notion of leveraged gains. You are most leveraged in the early years of your mortgage, so that is when you are most likely to see your gains magnified by leverage. But at that juncture, you are also paying the most mortgage interest, which reduces your net gain from owning the house.

Moreover, if you do sell your house quickly with a view to locking in any gain you have scored, transaction costs could wreak havoc with your returns. It is bad enough that you have to pay 6 percent to a broker if you sell a house after 30 years. But if you are selling homes every six or seven years, it is really tough to make money.

Also, bear in mind that leverage can cut both ways. In the example above, I assumed that your home's price increased. But there is no guarantee that your home's value will appreciate, especially if you own the place for just a few years. What if prices drop? The leveraged gains you were counting on could turn into leveraged losses. If your $150,000 home dropped to $120,000, your initial $30,000 in home equity would be obliterated.

So why do so many folks believe that they can make money from home-price appreciation? Much of it, I believe, is a holdover from the 1970s. The rampant inflation of that decade drove property prices higher. But pretty much everything else also went up, including wages, gas prices, and the cost of consumer goods. In this rising tide of prices, however, one key item got left behind. While home values were rising along with inflation, the amount that homeowners owed the bank stayed the same. That truly is a recipe for wealth.

Assume once more that you bought a $150,000 house with a $30,000 down payment. If all prices doubled, including home prices, your $150,000 house would suddenly be worth $300,000. Your home hasn't increased in value, once you figure in inflation. But your home equity has soared. After netting out the $120,000 owed to the bank, your equity has gone from $30,000 to $180,000.

In the 1970s, homeowners really did enjoy wonderful leveraged gains. But it wasn't because home-price appreciation is some miraculous source of wealth. It was because inflation was out of control. Will inflation spin out of control again? Don't count on it. Lately, among economists, the big worry has been deflation.

YIELDING TO REASON

This is the good-cop–bad-cop chapter. Once you rip off the rose-colored glasses and look at the real costs, it turns out that most homeowners won't make much money from home-price appreciation. But homes can still be a great investment.

For starters, when it comes to your home, you will probably behave like a long-term investor. You may be tempted to panic and sell when the stock market plunges. But you will happily tough it out with your home, waiting for its price to bounce back. Partly, that is because you don't really know what your home is worth until you go to sell it. On any given day, you can calculate the precise value of your stock funds. But your house might easily fetch $25,000 more or less than you imagine it is worth.

The tenacity of homeowners also reflects a greater sense of value. When you buy stocks and stock funds, you become part owners of often-thriving businesses. But these investments can seem like nothing more than numbers on an account statement. By contrast, with a home, it is easy to see what you own and to have some sense of its value.

In addition, owning a home forces you to save through month after month of mortgage payments. It may be a very costly way to save, thanks to all the mortgage interest. Still, unlike other investments, which are easy to blow off, this is one check that you have to write every month. Moreover, there are handsome tax advantages. Not only can you deduct your mortgage interest, but also you probably won't owe any capital-gains taxes when you sell.

All this stuff is penny ante, however, compared to the biggest advantage of all. What is that? Forget making money from the price appreciation. Forget the tax benefits. Forget the forced savings. The real advantage of homeownership is far more prosaic: You can live in the place.

Think of your house as a high-yielding stock. The capital gain is likely to be modest, maybe one percentage point a year more than inflation, and any gain could be wiped out by the costs you incur. But the dividend is huge. Stop for a moment and think about how much you could collect each year if you rented out your house. This sum might amount to 8 percent of your home's value, equal to $12,000 a year on a $150,000 home.

In all likelihood, however, you don't rent out your house. Instead, you live in your own home and effectively rent to yourself. Your dividend takes the form of what economists call "imputed rent." That rent, however, is still enormously valuable. In fact, renting to yourself is a smart tax strategy. If you let somebody else use your home, you would have to pay income taxes on the rent you collect. But when you live in your own home, you don't have to pay taxes on the imputed rent you receive.

Tote up the numbers and homes look pretty attractive. If your house appreciates at 4 percent annually and you tack on 8 percent for the dividend, you are looking at a 12 percent total return. Even after you back out 3 percent for inflation and a hefty sum for all costs, including maintenance, taxes, and mortgage interest, your home should still prove to be a fine investment.

In all this, you might quibble with my reasoning, wondering why I deduct all costs from a home's price appreciation, rather than subtracting these expenses from the dividend. Either way, you end up with the same total return.

Nonetheless, when analyzing your home's return, I

think it makes sense to subtract your housing costs from your capital gain. You incur insurance, maintenance expenses, property taxes, and mortgage costs, whether you use your house or not. Thus, it seems logical that these expenses should be deducted first from any price appreciation.

By running the numbers this way, I also hope to highlight a key lesson: To make good money from a house, you need to maximize the rent, whether by getting in a steady stream of tenants or by making full use of the place yourself. If you do that, the return can be mighty impressive.

Yet many people take this fine investment and manage to mess up royally. Where do they go wrong? It comes down to a fundamental misunderstanding of real estate. They think that the game is all about price appreciation. But in truth, the big money comes from the dividend. Grasp that concept and you start to understand the flawed thinking behind three popular real-estate strategies. What are the three strategies? Homeowners try to make money by fixing up their home, by trading up to a larger house, and by buying vacation properties for their own use. But all three strategies are likely to be financial dead ends.

HARDLY AN IMPROVEMENT

Let us start with one of my favorite pieces of real-estate foolishness, which is to try to make money by fixing up your house. As the stock-market slump drags on, some homeowners have apparently yanked money out of stocks and used the proceeds to fix up their homes. But that isn't likely to be a big moneymaker.

As I mentioned above, historically homes have appreciated at a little over one percentage point a year faster than inflation. To earn that return, you need to keep your home in decent shape. That means periodically replacing the roof, painting the house, repairing the plumbing, putting in a new furnace, and so on. These maintenance expenses might cost you between 1 and 2 percent of your home's value each year. This is, as they say, the price of doing business. If you don't maintain your home, you won't even earn that one percentage point a year more than inflation.

Most of us, however, aren't satisfied with mere maintenance. We also want to improve our homes, whether it is by upgrading the kitchen, finishing the basement, remodeling the bathrooms, or adding a deck. All of these projects can make our homes much more enjoyable places to live. But right there, you can see the flaw in much of the thinking about home improvements.

If you make your home a more enjoyable place to live, you have bolstered the value of your home's dividend. Have tenants in your home? You might now be able to charge more in rent. But what if you live in the house yourself? You have increased the amount of imputed rent you collect, because you now get more enjoyment from living in the house. Without a doubt, more imputed rent is a great thing. But it won't make you rich.

Of course, you could get rich if your home is now worth a whole lot more. And your home improvements will boost your home's value. But that increase in value is likely to be far less than the sum you spent. Partly, that is because potential buyers may not share your taste in home improvements. In addition, these improvements will deteriorate over time.

For proof, consider the annual survey in *Remodeling* magazine (www.remodeling.hw.net). In its cost-vs.-value survey, the magazine looks at how much you might recoup from various popular home improvements. Typically, homeowners get back 70 to 80 cents for every $1 they spend. The other 20 to 30 cents? That's gone.

These numbers may, in truth, paint too rosy a picture. *Remodeling* magazine bases its figures on estimates from real-estate agents and appraisers. For its November 2002 issue, *Consumer Reports* tried the same thing, but instead stuck only with real-estate appraisers. These appraisers figured that homeowners would typically recoup 40 to 75 cents of every $1 lavished on home improvements.

Both *Consumer Reports*' and *Remodeling*'s calculations are based on selling your home within a year of making the improvements. The longer you wait to sell, the shabbier your home improvements will look and thus the less you are likely to recoup. Your dividend from your home improvements is also likely to shrink over time. When you first remodeled your bathroom, you probably got a lot of pleasure from the spanking new fixtures and the shiny tiles. Three years later, when the fixtures no longer sparkle and the grout looks a little discolored, your pleasure is likely somewhat diminished.

For homeowners, there are two lessons here: First, don't fix up your home simply to increase its value. You should only undertake those improvements where the enjoyment you receive is commensurate with the dollars spent. That doesn't, however, mean that you should ignore financial considerations.

For instance, there may be some danger in remodeling your house to the point where it is far more lavish than anything else in the neighborhood. If you do that, there is a chance that you could recoup little or none of the money spent. Instead, home improvements make the most financial sense if you are fixing up your house so that it is comparable with other homes in the neighborhood.

What if your home-improvement ambitions are greater than that? Instead of fixing up your current home, you may want to buy a grander place. Which brings us to our second lesson: If you are in the market for a house, consider buying a place that has already been fixed up. Clearly, you will want a house that has been remodeled to your liking. But if you can find the right place, you may be able to purchase the owner's costly improvements at a steep discount.

BIGGER ISN'T BETTER

So maybe home improvements aren't a great investment. Next up, we have our second dubious strategy: Dumping your stocks and using the proceeds to trade up to a bigger house.

At first blush, that might seem like a sensible move. If home prices climb 100 percent over the next 17 or 18 years, which seems like a reasonable possibility, you will make more in dollar terms if you own a bigger house. Or will you? Go back to the start of this chapter, where we discussed the costs of homeownership and how these costs can cancel out any gain from home-price appreciation.

If you double the size of your house, you may double your dollar gain from rising home prices. But you will also likely double your maintenance expenses, monthly mortgage payment, taxes, and insurance costs. And when you trade up to the bigger place, not only will you get dinged for selling your current home, but also you will face a fistful of closing costs when buying your new, bigger house.

The numbers might seem more attractive if you don't need to take out a mortgage to buy the bigger home. Without the drag of mortgage-borrowing costs, you could make slightly more each year from your home's price appreciation than you lose to costs. But your gain will still be pretty measly. If you compare this performance to the return from a low-cost short-term bond fund, it is no contest. Pouring the extra money into a bigger house looks like a real loser.

Except, of course, that you can't live in a short-term bond fund. You can live in your house. Yet again, we are back to the critical distinction between the dividend and the capital gain. If you trade up to a bigger house, you are unlikely to make much from the price appreciation, once you figure in the higher costs involved. But as with home improvements, you are increasing your real-estate dividend. Thus, you need to ask yourself a key question: Will you get sufficient pleasure from the bigger house to make trading up worthwhile?

If the answer is no, you should stick with your current home. If you won't appreciate the higher dividend, you are throwing your money away. It is the equivalent of renting a suite at a hotel and then spending all your time in just one room. You would be much better off renting a smaller room and using the extra cash for something else.

On the other hand, if you will really enjoy the larger house, by all means consider trading up. Keep three things in mind, however. First, try to keep the transaction costs involved to a minimum. Instead of paying the standard 6 percent commission, see if you can get your broker to accept 5 or even $4\frac{1}{2}$ percent to sell your current home.

Second, think carefully about how you structure the mortgage on your new home. If you have already paid off a big chunk of the 30-year mortgage on your old house, you are effectively starting the mortgage clock all over again if you take out another 30-year loan. What's the alternative? You might want to opt for a 15-year loan, even though that will mean a larger monthly payment.

But before you sign up for the shorter loan, think about whether you can handle the higher monthly payments. What if you get laid off? Your newly acquired mansion may suddenly seem like a millstone. If you are not certain that your job is secure, I would apply for another 30-year mortgage to keep your monthly financial obligations small. If you later decide you want to shorten the length of your mortgage, you can always make extra-principal payments.

Finally, we come to our most critical issue. Can you afford the luxury of a bigger house? Yes, by trading up, you will collect a bigger dividend. But unless you rent out a few rooms in your new, larger house, that bigger dividend won't be of the cash variety. Rather, you are the one consuming the bigger dividend. Should you be devoting so much money to an investment that won't deliver any sort of cash return? If you are struggling to amass enough for retirement, you probably ought to stick with your current home and instead use the extra money to fatten your investment portfolio.

SECOND TO NONE

Rather than trading up to a bigger house or embarking on lavish home improvements, some people have dumped stocks and used the money to buy vacation homes. A smart move? If you have followed the gist of my argument, you will immediately see the flaw with this third strategy.

My fear is that folks will buy a second home, use the property themselves and then hope to make money from the capital gain. But as I have indicated above, this is a sure route to mediocre returns. After all costs, you are unlikely to make much from a vacation home's price appreciation. In addition, if you have to take on some sort of mortgage, you are hiking your fixed monthly costs and thus crimping your financial flexibility.

What if you buy a vacation home, rent it out, and collect your dividend in cold cash? In that case, you could indeed make decent money. You will have to pay incomes taxes on the rent you receive. But even after Uncle Sam gets his cut, you should still notch a healthy gain. Nonetheless, I have a few misgivings about buying rental properties. You are making a big bet on a single property market. What if the market turns in lackluster returns, with property prices failing to keep up with inflation? Even if you manage to earn a steady stream of rent, you may end up with uninspiring results, thanks to stagnant property prices.

To ensure that you don't end up with a lemon, pick your property carefully. People sometimes quip that land is a great investment, because they aren't making any more of it. But that is not true of houses. Everywhere you turn, they are slapping together the two-by-fours. Keep that in mind when considering whether to purchase a vacation property.

Looking to buy a place near a ski resort or in a wilderness location, where there is still a heap of undeveloped land that could one day be covered with condominiums and vacation cottages? The odds are, homes in the area will be a poor investment, because there is a potentially large supply of new housing. Instead, you will probably fare better if you buy a house in, say, a well-developed seaside town. They may still be putting up a few new homes. But the amount of shoreline isn't likely to grow.

Even if you find the right property, there are other drawbacks to consider. What if the economy takes a turn for the worse and you have trouble renting your second home? If you are relying on rent to help pay the property's mortgage, you could find yourself in a nasty financial squeeze.

Moreover, being a landlord is no fun. Think about all those whiny tenants. Think about the damage they might do. Think about hassling them to pay the rent on time. Just thinking about it makes me reach for the Tylenol. This is why I much prefer stocks and bonds to real estate. Yes, you have to sit there day after day, watching your stocks and bonds fluctuate in value. But at least stocks and bonds don't call you up in the middle of the night, complaining that the furnace is broken.

STOCKING UP ON REAL ESTATE

Don't get me wrong. I am not writing off real estate as an investment. As it turns out, you can invest in real estate without purchasing actual properties. How? It is time to consider real-estate investment trusts, often known as REITs.

Real-estate investment trusts have been around since the 1960s, but their numbers have grown rapidly over the past decade. Some REITs only lend money to property developers. Other REITs both buy properties and lend out money. But the vast majority of REITS focus exclusively on purchasing properties and then renting them out. If you want returns that track the real-estate market, consider investing in these so-called equity REITs.

Equity REITs tend to specialize. Some focus on a particular part of the country. Some focus on particular types of property, such as shopping malls, hotels, warehouses, or apartment buildings. Each type will fare slightly differently depending, in part, on where we are in the economic cycle. Hotels tend to suffer more during recessions, because their tenants rent by the day. Meanwhile, office buildings and industrial properties are steadier businesses, because their tenants are locked into multiyear leases.

Part of the attraction of REITs lies in their special tax

status. A REIT doesn't have to pay tax on the income it passes along to shareholders. But to get this exemption, a REIT must distribute at least 90 percent of its taxable income each year as dividends. Most REITs, in fact, distribute 100 percent of their taxable income and sometimes more.

Investment advisers used to argue that investors didn't need REITs in their portfolio, because anybody who currently owned a house already had plenty of real-estate exposure. After strong gains by REITs in 2000 and 2001, you don't hear this argument anymore. Amazing how that happens, isn't it? While other people may find REITs more alluring after their recent heady gains, this spurt of great performance makes me a little nervous. Moreover, if Congress makes dividends from other stocks partially or entirely tax-free, REITs may lose some of their attraction, because their dividends wouldn't be covered by this tax break.

Still, even though REITs aren't as appealing as they were in early 2000, I think that there is a decent chance that they will post healthy gains in the decade ahead. Remember the last chapter, where I suggested that this could turn out to be the decade of the dividend and the interest payment? REITs are another high-yielding investment that should sparkle in a low-return environment.

With a home, most of your gain comes from the dividend, with relatively little from capital gains. Not surprisingly, the same pattern holds true with REITs. According to the National Association of Real Estate Investment Trusts in Washington, D.C., equity REITs have returned 12.5 percent a year since 1971, versus 12.2 percent for the Standard & Poor's 500-stock index. But for

REITs, the share-price gains have been relatively modest. Instead, the bulk of the return has come from dividends.

Lately, REITs have been yielding around 7 percent. If you collect that dividend, while REIT share prices climb along with inflation, you should garner an annual return of maybe 9 or 10 percent. That seems pretty attractive, especially compared with the 5 or 6 percent available on corporate bonds and an estimated 8 percent from a globally diversified stock portfolio.

Fidelity, T. Rowe Price, and TIAA–CREF offer actively managed no-load REIT funds with annual expenses of 1 percent or less. But if you prefer index funds, the only current choice for small investors is the Vanguard REIT Index Fund, which has a $3,000 investment minimum and annual expenses of just 0.28 percent. Because much of the return from REITs takes the form of immediately taxable income, consider holding your REIT fund in a retirement account.

What percentage of your portfolio should you invest in REITs? This is a tricky one. REITs are a tiny part of the stock market, with a combined market value of some $160 billion. That means that REITs account for less than 2 percent of the U.S. stock market. But I think investors should seriously consider putting much more than that percentage in REITs.

The fact is, most real estate isn't owned by REITs. The value of all commercial and residential U.S. real estate is estimated at some $24 trillion, while the value of all stocks in late 2002 was around $10 trillion. My advice: You might put as much as 10 percent of your stock portfolio in real-estate investment trusts, and really aggressive investors could go as high as 15 percent.

6 WORKING TOWARD RETIREMENT

"Seven Stocks to Buy Now," screams the magazine cover. "25 Great Ways to Invest $1,000," hollers the headline. "The One Retirement Strategy You Need Now," promises the article.

If only it were that easy.

There is, I regret, no magic bullet. There is no one right thing that, if done, will ensure your financial future. Salvation doesn't lie in technology stocks, or market timing, or rental real estate, or the third race at Pimlico. Instead, if you want to retire in comfort, you will need to do a lot of things right. We have already talked about some of those things. Consider stock-index funds. Diversify globally. Favor low-cost bond funds. Add high-yield junk bonds. Buy real-estate investment trusts.

These are all key ingredients in your investment strategy. But how do you bring all of these ingredients together to build a winning portfolio? To make your strategy work, you will need to settle on the right mix of stocks, bonds, and real estate, save like crazy, make full use of retirement accounts, and get time on your side. Want more details? Read on.

MIXING IT UP

In the 1990s, different market sectors posted radically different investment results. According to Ibbotson Associates, the blue-chip stocks in the Standard & Poor's 500 index climbed an average 18.2 percent a year, small U.S. stocks returned 15.1 percent, high-yield junk bonds 10.7 percent, real-estate investment trusts 9.1 percent, long-term corporate bonds 8.4 percent, and foreign stocks 7.3 percent. Meanwhile, inflation checked in at 2.9 percent annually.

Over the decade ahead, I suspect that the range of returns will be much tighter, with a mix of high-quality corporate and government bonds delivering around 5 percent, the S&P 500 muddling along at 8 percent, and other parts of the global stock market clocking 9 or 10 percent. What does that mean for your portfolio? There are, I believe, three major implications.

First, taking risk will still be rewarded, but not to nearly the degree that it has been historically. In the past, if you wanted to boost your portfolio's long-run return, you could simply move a little money out of bonds and into stocks. That strategy should still work, but the additional return may be relatively modest.

This is good news for risk-averse investors. In the past, adding bonds to a stock portfolio has been a notably mixed blessing. Sure, you reduced risk. But you also greatly reduced your returns. In the years ahead, however, you may not pay much of a performance penalty for favoring bonds. As I indicated in Chapter 4, the outlook for Treasury bonds isn't great. But high-quality corporate bonds may only lag behind stocks by two or three percentage points a year, while high-yield junk bonds could do as well as stocks and possibly better.

Second, if you are like most stock investors and lean toward blue-chip U.S. shares, you will need to be more adventurous. True, these blue-chip stocks were the top performers of the 1990s. But past isn't prologue. You would be smart to diversify into small stocks, foreign markets, and real-estate investment trusts. It is not simply that these investments will provide valuable diversification. In addition, they may outperform blue-chip stocks, thus bolstering your portfolio's return.

Third, the decade ahead may offer a great chance to goose your portfolio's performance through rebalancing. I believe that rebalancing is one of the most underappreciated investment techniques. As you might recall from Chapter 2, if you diversify among various market sectors, you can reduce your portfolio's risk level, without reducing its return. For that reason, diversification is sometimes described as Wall Street's only free lunch.

Rebalancing takes that free lunch and makes it taste a whole lot better. How? Rebalancing brings discipline to the diversification process. It forces you to set target percentages for each investment and then to adjust your holdings on a regular basis, thereby getting your portfolio back into line with these target weights. For instance, if you have earmarked 5 percent of your stock portfolio for emerging markets and those markets take a hit, you should add money to the sector to boost your portfolio weighting back up to 5 percent.

If you can, try to rebalance by directing fresh savings to underweighted areas. This makes particular sense if you are investing in a taxable account, where moving money from one fund to another could trigger a tax bill.

But in your retirement account, taxes aren't an issue. There, you don't have to worry that your trading will trigger capital-gains taxes. As a result, you can get your portfolio back into balance by shifting money from one fund to another.

Traditionally, rebalancing has been pitched as a risk-reduction strategy. Suppose you settle on a mix of 60 percent stocks and 40 percent bonds. Every year or so, you might check your stock–bond mix to see if it is still in line with those targets. If stocks have fared especially well over the prior 12 months and are now at, say, 64 percent of your portfolio's total value, you would look to bolster your bond holdings, either by directing fresh savings to bonds or by selling stocks and using the proceeds to buy bonds. That has the effect of keeping your portfolio's risk level under control.

In the past, however, rebalancing between stocks and bonds has also tended to reduce returns, because you were usually compelled to sell stocks, which have been the best-performing asset over the long haul. Indeed, if you wanted the highest possible long-run return, you would never rebalance your mix of stocks and bonds.

But rebalancing doesn't always crimp returns. As I noted in Chapter 3, rebalancing among different stock-market sectors has the potential to both reduce risk and boost performance. How so? When rebalancing, you are buying low and selling high. Rebalancing forces you to throttle back on sectors that have lately done well and to add to those that are suffering. If different stock sectors generate similar long-run returns, this rebalancing should lead to higher long-run performance.

Now, think about returns for the decade ahead. If all

investments are likely to generate fairly similar long-run returns, rebalancing could turn out to be a great strategy over the next 10 years. And I'm not talking just about re-balancing among different stock-market sectors. If high-quality and high-yield corporate bonds post returns that aren't significantly different from those generated by the blue-chip stocks in the S&P 500, investors may be able to reduce their portfolio's risk by adding these bonds, without greatly hurting returns.

It all has to do with the rebalancing bonus. The performance gain that comes from rebalancing between stocks and bonds may compensate for the lower results delivered by bonds. Moreover, you should get plenty of chances to put the strategy into practice. Stocks and bonds often go in different directions, thus offering frequent opportunities to rebalance.

The same is also true of real estate, which moves in its own cycle, separate from both stocks and bonds. If you want to collect a rebalancing bonus from real estate, you should favor real-estate investment trusts over rental real estate. After all, you can't buy or sell slivers of your vacation home to get your real-estate exposure back to your target percentage. But it is easy to tweak your REIT holdings.

Incidentally, rebalancing is also the key to squeezing good returns out of precious-metals mutual funds, which make their money by investing mostly in gold-mining companies. Investors often buy these funds as a hedge against calamity, because gold stocks tend to post gains when other investments are getting hammered. The problem is, the long-run return from a precious-metals mutual fund is likely to be mediocre. But here's the surprise: Despite those mediocre long-run results, a gold fund doesn't have to be a big drag on your portfolio's performance.

Because gold's pattern of performance is so different from that of other investments, you can garner a handsome rebalancing bonus if you allocate maybe 3 percent of your portfolio to a precious-metals mutual fund and then regularly buy and sell gold to keep it at this target percentage. That rebalancing bonus can take a precious-metals fund, with its lackluster long-run results, and turn it into a decent contributor to your portfolio's overall performance.

Put all these various funds together and what sort of mix might you have? In the two accompanying pie charts, I have put together a couple of model portfolios. But there is nothing magical about these mixes. If you want greater simplicity, you could collapse some of the categories.

You might, for instance, skip separate holdings for large stocks and small stocks, and instead buy a total–stock-market index fund that tracks the Wilshire 5000 or the Russell 3000. Alternatively, you could specialize even more, splitting your large- and small-stock holdings between growth and value funds. Also, don't feel compelled to replicate the percentages I have used. You could stick with the investments shown, but raise or lower the percentage allocations, depending on which investments you are most comfortable with.

But whatever you do, there are two keys. First, you want to own a relatively broad mix of funds, so that you are well diversified and have plenty of chances to rebalance. Second, once you settle on target percentages for your various funds, you have to stick with them. All the market sectors included in the pie charts will generate decent returns over time. But you will never collect those decent returns if you invest heavily in a sector and then panic and sell at the worst possible moment.

More cautious investors should clearly favor the conservative mix, while those with an appetite for risk might opt for the aggressive mix. But how do you know if you are conservative or aggressive? This is a great time to gauge your risk tolerance. You have just lived through one of the all-time worst bear markets. Did you take it in stride or did you suffer sleepless nights? Use your reaction to guide your portfolio building, especially when deciding how to split your portfolio between stocks and bonds.

Once you have built your new portfolio, settle on a schedule for rebalancing. As a rule, I would look to rebalance once a year. Investors, I believe, fare best when they follow strict rules, rather than leaving matters to intuition. Still, when it comes to rebalancing, you may want to be a little flexible.

A number of academic studies have found that there is momentum in stock returns. Investments that post big

AGGRESSIVE INVESTORS

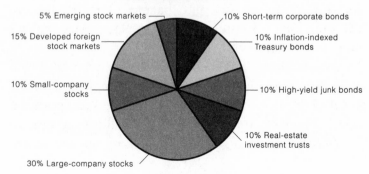

5% Emerging stock markets

15% Developed foreign stock markets

10% Small-company stocks

30% Large-company stocks

10% Short-term corporate bonds

10% Inflation-indexed Treasury bonds

10% High-yield junk bonds

10% Real-estate investment trusts

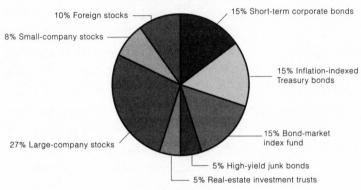

CONSERVATIVE INVESTORS

10% Foreign stocks

8% Small-company stocks

15% Short-term corporate bonds

15% Inflation-indexed Treasury bonds

15% Bond-market index fund

27% Large-company stocks

5% High-yield junk bonds

5% Real-estate investment trusts

gains one year often do better than average in the year that follows. As a consequence, you might benefit by rebalancing once every two years. On the other hand, we also occasionally get big short-term market moves. For instance, stock-market sectors sometimes lose 10 percent or more in a matter of days. These big moves can throw your portfolio's weights far out of whack and thus rebalancing may be in order.

Rebalancing in the midst of such market mayhem can be both nerve-racking and comforting. After you have seen a sector drop 20, 30, or even 50 percent, it is tough to step up to the plate and buy more, in order to get your portfolio back into balance. For that reason, you shouldn't allocate more to a sector than you are truly comfortable with.

But while rebalancing can leave your stomach churning, it can also ease some of the anguish of a market decline. It is tough to sit tight, while your portfolio gets pummeled. At times of crisis, we all get the urge to act. Rebalancing can give you something sensible to do.

SOCKING IT AWAY

One rule of thumb suggests that your retirement spending might run at 75 or 80 percent of your pre-retirement level. The notion is that you don't need quite as much spending money once you are retired, because you won't have commuting costs anymore, there is no need to buy office clothes, and you should be able to live somewhat more thriftily.

I consider this rule of thumb to be all but useless. The reality is, once you are retired, a lot of costs don't go away and some are likely to jump sharply. If you spend 20 or 30 years in retirement, you will need to replace the roof at least once, you might buy a couple of cars, and there will be the usual array of unexpected expenses. It could be that, even in retirement, you are still paying off your mortgage.

To make matters worse, once you are retired, the temptations to spend are huge. Think about how much money you burn through during a one-week vacation. Now, imagine being on vacation for 52 weeks a year. If you are not careful, you could easily find yourself spending more than you did prior to retirement.

In short, retirement isn't cheap. How can you make sure that you have enough money? It is hardly the greatest financial insight or the most sophisticated advice. But let us be realistic: To retire in comfort, you will have to save like crazy. Shooting for higher returns is an iffy proposition. But if you save more each month, your portfolio will definitely grow faster. Indeed, if you are approaching retirement and you don't have much of a nest egg, saving heaps of money is the key to a comfortable retirement. At that stage, building a finely calibrated portfolio and rebalancing regularly will help, but it won't help a whole lot. Instead, if you are close to age sixty-five, what counts is socking away every penny that you can.

As we can all attest, this isn't easy. We are just not good at delaying gratification. Yes, we know that we need to save for our future. But no, we would rather not start today. In the battle for self-control, we often end up on the losing side. What to do? If you want to get yourself to save, you will need to use the full arsenal of silly tricks and psychological gamesmanship. Here are six strategies that should help:

1. **Save something.** I don't care how much you save or how you start. But get started. Grab an old jar and stick $2 in it every evening. Steal your kid's piggybank and fill it with all the coins you collect during the course of the day. When you balance your checkbook, round down the sum to the nearest dollar, so you have a growing invisible balance in your bank account. Once you have amassed a small sum, use it to open a savings account.

   Stupid? You had better believe it. But that first step is often the hardest, so do whatever it takes. I would get that savings account opened, even if it means carrying credit-card debt that is costing you far more than your savings account will earn. You need to see your savings start to grow. Once you see that and you get some sense of financial progress, your enthusiasm will likely increase and you will want to save even more each month.

   At this juncture, time really is money. If the bear market has savaged your nest egg, it is critical that you get a quick start on your savings program. That way, you will have more time to save and more time for those savings to earn investment returns, and together those advantages will snowball in your favor.

Consider an example. If you are age forty and you sock away $5,000 every year, you will have over $316,000 at age sixty-five. This figure assumes that you earn a 7 percent annual return, but it ignores inflation and taxes. What if you wait until age forty-five to start saving? You could still accumulate that $316,000 by age sixty-five. But to amass that sum, you will have to save over $7,700 every year, or 54 percent more.

2. **Reap windfalls.** As you try to bolster your savings rate, you may initially find it tough to squeeze money out of your regular paycheck. But it is relatively easy to save financial windfalls. These windfalls take all forms.

Maybe it is overtime pay, the insurance reimbursement for a medical bill, a tax refund, a year-end bonus, money from a second job, an inheritance, or the daycare reimbursement from the dependent-care account you have at work. It seems like less of a sacrifice to save this money, because this money isn't part of your regular income. Just received a windfall? Add that to your nest egg.

3. **Challenge yourself.** Spare change and financial windfalls will carry you only so far. You have to start carving out a decent chunk of your regular paycheck and socking it away every month. The problem is, it is hard to save just for the sake of saving money. You

are much more likely to make the necessary sacrifices if you really want that bigger house, or for your daughter to go to Princeton, or to quit the work force at age sixty-two. Setting goals supplies both the reason and the incentive to save.

But don't just think about how much money you would like to have at age sixty-two. Also think about how much you want to sock away by the end of the year. Set a monthly savings target. Commit to saving a portion of this week's paycheck. That challenge should spur you to cut spending and save more.

4. **Give at the office.** Everybody can find ways to pare their spending. Maybe you can eat out less, quit smoking, take less lavish vacations, cut back on your clothing budget, or go cold turkey on lottery tickets. But finding items to cut is the easy part. So what's the hitch? If you try to scale back your spending and then save whatever remains, you will struggle constantly with temptation.

The solution is not only to set savings goals, but also to remove the choice to spend. You need to force yourself to save, and the best way to do that is by signing up to participate in your employer's 401(k) or 403(b) retirement-savings program. With these plans, your contributions come straight out of your paycheck, so the money is gone before you get a chance to spend it.

In addition to providing a useful dose of financial discipline, these plans are also typically the best place to stash your savings. Why? Your contributions are usually tax-deductible, they will grow tax-deferred, and you may get some sort of matching contribution from your employer.

5. **Do it automatically.** Like the idea of forced savings? You can employ the same strategy outside of your employer's plan, by using mutual-fund automatic-investment plans. With these plans, you can arrange for $50 or $100 to be removed from your bank account every month and invested directly into the mutual funds you choose. Not only does this overcome the temptation to spend, but it also offers a cheap way to get started in funds.

   Fund companies such as T. Rowe Price Associates, TIAA–CREF, and USAA will waive their regular mutual-fund investment minimums if you sign up for an automatic investment plan of $50 or more per month. Be warned: TIAA–CREF charges an annual $25 low-balance fee if your account is below $1,500. But you can avoid that fee by committing to an automatic investment plan of at least $100 a month.

   When you buy stock funds using automatic-investment plans or payroll deduction into a 401(k) or 403(b) plan, you end up employing the stock-market buying technique known as dollar-cost averaging. With dollar-cost averaging, the idea is to invest a fixed sum every month, no matter what is happening to share prices. Dollar-cost averaging can help you make money, even if stocks don't post strong gains.

   Suppose that you invest $100 in a stock fund every month. In the first month, the fund's shares are at $10, which means your $100 buys 10 shares. The following month, the share price plunges to $5, so your $100 buys 20 shares. Next, the share price bounces back to $7.50, halfway between your two purchase prices. Back to even? In fact, at $7.50 a share, you have a profit. Your 30 shares, for which you paid $200, are now worth $225.

Impressed? The math works out that way because you are investing a fixed-dollar amount each month. Result: You buy more shares when the price is down, which has the effect of sharply reducing the average price paid. Indeed, if you increase your monthly investment as share prices fall, the numbers can be even more impressive.

But don't get too hung up on the math. The real benefit of dollar-cost averaging is, I believe, psychological. It is tough to start investing in the stock market, because there is always that fear that the market is currently "too high." Spooning money into the market removes such worries. Dollar-cost averaging can also make you a more tenacious investor. When the market rises, you have the pleasure of getting richer. When share prices fall, you know that your next monthly investment will buy shares at cheaper prices.

6. **Lend a hand.** As I noted in Chapter 5, many folks say that their home is the best investment they ever made. Owning a home forces you to save. You have to make those monthly mortgage payments or you will be out on the street. But if the regular mortgage payment is good, maybe a little more is even better.

Why not write a slightly larger check and thus pay down your loan more quickly? Like automatic investment plans and payroll deduction into an employer-sponsored retirement account, your monthly mortgage check offers a great opportunity to develop good financial habits.

The return you get from paying down your mortgage probably won't be as handsome as that from investing in stock funds or plunking money in a tax-deductible retirement account. But if you are a conservative investor who favors certificates of deposit and bonds, the return from prepaying a mortgage can be attractive.

If you follow the six strategies above, you will soon be carving out a hefty percentage of your monthly income and socking it away for the future. Thanks to your mortgage, 401(k), and automatic investment plans, saving will no longer be a choice. Instead of trying to spend less so that you can save more, you will be forced to save first and then live on whatever remains. But there is always the risk of backsliding. Maybe, even as you salt away money with one hand, you will withdraw it with the other, by taking a loan from your employer's retirement plan or borrowing against your home equity.

We all get into tight spots occasionally and need to borrow money. But it is not a habit you want to develop. With that in mind, try to make your home and your investments psychologically untouchable. To some degree, you probably do this already. Often, people are more than happy to spend money that is in their bank account, but deeply reluctant to dip into retirement accounts, tap home equity, or touch money held at brokerage firms or mutual-fund companies. But once you break these prohibitions, they are tough to resurrect, so

I wouldn't take out a home-equity or 401(k) loan unless it is a dire emergency.

If you do develop good savings habits, you won't just find it easier to amass money for retirement. You will also reduce the amount you need in retirement. Imagine two families with the same income. But one family saves just 5 percent of their income, while the other saves 20 percent. The family that saves less will obviously be used to a much higher level of spending, which means that they will need a much bigger nest egg to maintain their current standard of living once they are retired.

TAKING SHELTER

Saving is a bargain and spending is expensive. Suppose that, after deducting Social Security payroll taxes, you have $1 of income. If you set out to spend that $1, you might lose 31 cents to federal and state income taxes and another four cents to sales taxes, leaving you with goods worth just 65 cents.

Now, imagine instead that you save that $1 in your employer's 401(k) plan. Your contribution is tax deductible, so you get to hang onto the full $1. Moreover, your employer might match your contribution at, say, 50 cents on the dollar. The bottom line? Instead of 65 cents of goods, you have $1.50 of savings, which will then go on to earn investment gains, so that it will eventually be worth $2, $3, or even more.

This example doesn't just illustrate the virtues of

thrift. It also highlights the importance of minimizing taxes. If you want to make your savings work hard, you should sock them away in as tax-savvy a manner as possible. Remember the snowball effect that comes from buying stock-index funds, favoring low-cost bond funds, and saving regularly? Ditto for taxes. Investing in a tax-efficient manner won't make much difference to your portfolio's performance in any given year. But over time, the impact can be huge.

I have already mentioned the great benefits of funding 401(k) and 403(b) plans, with their initial tax deduction, employer match, and tax-deferred growth. Make no mistake: These plans are the sweetest deal in savings. Thanks to the 2001 tax law, you will be able to stuff even more dollars into these accounts in the years ahead. The maximum you can contribute to 401(k) and 403(b) plans rises from $12,000 in 2003 to $15,000 in 2006. The annual contribution limits are even higher for those age fifty and older. These folks, who can contribute $14,000 in 2003, will be able to invest $20,000 by 2006.

Similarly, the contribution limits for regular and Roth individual retirement accounts are also slated to increase. The current $3,000 annual limit rises to $4,000 in 2005 and $5,000 in 2008. Those fifty and older can invest an extra $500 currently and an additional $1,000 starting in 2006.

Occasionally, I hear investors argue that it isn't worth funding tax-deductible individual retirement accounts. These detractors point out that everything withdrawn from an individual retirement account gets taxed as ordinary income, even if the account's growth was the result of capital gains. Meanwhile, if these capital gains occurred in a regular taxable account, they would be taxed at the lower capital-gains tax rate.

For instance, suppose you are in the 27 percent federal income-tax bracket. If you earn a long-term capital gain in your taxable account, it will be taxed at 20 percent or possibly just 18 percent. But the same capital gain in an IRA will be dunned at the 27 percent income-tax rate. Thus, with the IRA, you seem to end up paying tax at an unnecessarily high rate.

This is true, but beside the point. To understand why, suppose that you invest $3,000 in a tax-deductible IRA. Thanks to the initial deduction, you would save $810 in taxes, assuming that you are in the 27 percent income-tax bracket. As a result, your out-of-pocket cost is just $2,190. Over the next 20 years, your $3,000 quadruples to $12,000. You then withdraw that $12,000, paying Uncle Sam 27 percent of that sum, or $3,240. As it happens, that $3,240 is exactly quadruple your initial tax savings of $810. In other words, your initial tax savings effectively pay for the final tax bill and thus your gain is essentially tax-free.

Sound appealing? As attractive as a tax-deductible IRA is, a Roth IRA can be even better. Currently, you can invest a total of $3,000 a year in all types of IRAs, or $3,500 if you are age fifty or older. But which should you fund: a Roth or a regular IRA?

With a regular IRA, you can get an initial tax deduction, but everything coming out in retirement is taxable as ordinary income. With a Roth, there is no initial tax deduction, but all withdrawals in retirement are tax-free. Put that way, choosing between a Roth and a regular IRA might seem like a toss-up. But in truth, for many people, the Roth will be the better bet. The explanation is a tad complex, so bear with me while I explain.

Suppose you and your brother are both in the 27 percent income-tax bracket. You invest $3,000 in a Roth, which grows to $30,000 over the next 30 years, at which point you withdraw the money tax-free in retirement. Meanwhile, your brother invests his $3,000 in a tax-deductible IRA, which also grows to $30,000. He withdraws the money in retirement, paying $8,100 in income taxes, because of his 27 percent tax bracket. That leaves him with just $21,900, versus $30,000 for your Roth. You would seem to be the winner.

But remember, your brother also had the initial $810 in tax savings from when he first funded his IRA. If your brother blows the $810 at the shopping mall, he won't have a chance of keeping up with your Roth. But let us assume that he is an avid saver and invests the $810. He can't stash the $810 in his IRA, because he has already contributed the maximum. Instead, he invests the $810 in a taxable account.

At that point, however, your brother is sunk. Even if he earned returns that were comparable to the returns garnered by his IRA, the $810 still wouldn't grow to $8,100 and cover his IRA's tax bill. Why not? For the $810 to grow to $8,100, it would have to grow entirely tax-free—and that isn't likely to happen with a taxable account. In effect, both a Roth and a regular IRA can give you tax-free gains. But the Roth gives you tax-free growth on the full $3,000, while the regular IRA will only give you tax-free growth on $2,190, assuming that you are in the 27 percent income-tax bracket.

Astute readers will note that I am making a big assumption, which is that your brother's tax rate stays the same. What if his tax rate drops sharply over the 30 years? In that case, your brother may be better off taking a tax deduction at today's higher rate and withdrawing 30 years from now and paying tax at a much lower rate.

But to be honest, predicting your tax rate is probably as dicey as trying to predict the stock market's short-term direction. It seems safer to assume that your tax rate won't change too much over the decades ahead. What if you do find yourself in a lower tax bracket in retirement? As you will discover in Chapter 7, there are some intriguing ways to exploit that. Trust me: That tax opportunity won't go to waste.

Still prefer the tax-deductible IRA? It may turn out that you aren't eligible and thus you have to plunk for the Roth. If you are covered by a retirement plan at work, you can't fully fund a tax-deductible IRA in 2003 unless you are single with adjusted gross income of less than $40,000 or are married filing jointly with combined income below $60,000. By contrast, you can fully fund a Roth if you are single with adjusted gross income below $95,000 or married filing jointly with income of less than $150,000.

If you do fund a Roth, you will find it has an unusual advantage. I hate to publicize this, because I don't like the notion of people tapping their retirement accounts early. But the fact is, you can withdraw your regular annual contributions from your Roth at any time.

Let's say that you invested $3,000 in a Roth every year for the next four years, for a total of $12,000. Usually, with a retirement account, if you tried to touch that money before age 59½, you would get slapped with tax penalties. But with a Roth IRA, you could pull out your $12,000 in contributions and owe nothing to Uncle Sam.

You would only trigger taxes and tax penalties if you withdrew the account's investment earnings. Thus, your Roth could act as a financial backstop, should you suddenly need a wad of cash.

What if you convert your traditional IRA to a Roth? That, too, will give you added financial flexibility. You can convert a regular IRA to a Roth only if your modified adjusted gross income during the year is less than $100,000; the sum converted doesn't count toward this $100,000 threshold.

In any case, if your income is above $100,000, you don't want to convert. Because you have to pay income taxes on the sum converted, you should convert only if your income is fairly modest that year and thus you are in a low tax bracket. Once you have moved money into a Roth and forked over the necessary conversion tax, your account will grow tax-free thereafter.

But what about that added financial flexibility? As with your regular annual contributions, you can withdraw the sum converted before age 59½. But to avoid a tax penalty on these withdrawals, there are two stipulations: First, you have to wait until the fifth year after the conversion. Second, you cannot withdraw the investment earnings that occur in the account after you make the conversion. To avoid getting dunned by Uncle Sam, you have to wait until retirement before tapping those investment earnings.

Whenever I write columns extolling the virtues of Roth IRAs, I get a fistful of e-mails from naysayers, who fret that Congress will renege on its promise and start taxing Roth withdrawals. I, of course, can't predict what Congress will do. But I suspect that, if Congress ever did move to tax Roth withdrawals, it would be as part of some surcharge that was applied to all retirement accounts and thus those with regular IRAs would be no better off.

As you line up the tax and other advantages of the various accounts on offer, it is pretty clear what you should do. Your top priority each year should be funding your employer's 401(k) or 403(b) plan. Next, you should stuff dollars into an IRA, preferably a Roth. If you have still more money to invest, you might pay down your mortgage, build up your taxable account, or purchase a tax-deferred fixed or variable annuity.

But which investments should you hold in each account? Start with your 401(k) or 403(b) and see what investment options are on offer. Suppose your employer's plan includes an S&P 500–stock index fund and some reasonably priced bond funds. If so, you might opt to buy those funds. But you may not find a small-company– or foreign-stock index fund in your 401(k) or 403(b). Your employer's plan probably also doesn't include an inflation-indexed bond fund, a real-estate fund, or a high-yield junk-bond fund.

As a consequence, you have to be creative. You might look to buy these other funds in your other accounts. For instance, you might use your IRA to hold tax-inefficient investments, such as a junk-bond fund, a real-estate fund, and an inflation-indexed bond fund. Meanwhile, in your taxable account, you might buy a foreign-stock index fund and a small-company–stock index fund.

But even small-company index funds can make surprisingly large capital-gains distributions each year. To reduce the tax hit, you might go for a more tax-efficient substitute, such as Vanguard's tax-managed small-stock fund. Alternatively, if your employer's plan offers an actively managed small-company fund, you might hold your nose and buy that fund.

By now, you have the outlines of your investment strategy. You have figured out what sort of portfolio mix you will hold. You know which funds you will use and whether you will hold these funds in your retirement account or your taxable account. You have decided how often you will rebalance and how much you will aim to save each month. Next, scribble down all these details on a scrap of paper and post it on the refrigerator.

This is your investment policy. Big institutional investors do the same thing. They may not scribble and they don't stick notes on the refrigerator. But they do essentially the same thing, drawing up investment policies that formalize their strategy. By writing down all these details, you force yourself to articulate your precise strategy for managing money, rather than relying on half-hearted commitments to save and vague notions of how to invest.

At times of panic, when you are tempted to throw everything out the window, go back and look at your investment policy. Like a nagging parent, your scribblings will remind you what strategy you fixed upon in calmer times. Maybe this will give you the fortitude to stick with your investments.

WORKING LATE

Even after the stock-market drubbing of the past three years, I believe most people should be able to retire by age sixty-five if they save diligently and invest intelligently. Imagine that you are age fifty and you haven't saved a nickel toward retirement. If you sock away $6,000 a year for the next 15 years and earn 7 percent a year while inflation runs at 3 percent, you will have $119,107 at age sixty-five, figured in today's dollars.

Doesn't sound like much? Suppose you stuck the entire sum in an immediate-fixed annuity. As you will learn in the next chapter, I wouldn't advise such an extreme strategy. But if you did plunk the full $119,107 in a fixed annuity, you could generate monthly income of maybe $825 if you are a man and $775 if you are a woman. The figure for women is lower, because annuity sellers know that women tend to live longer and thus sellers will likely have to make those monthly payments for longer.

Keep in mind that, when you go to buy an immediate annuity, you may be offered monthly income that is significantly higher or lower than these sums. The monthly income offered to new immediate-annuity buyers fluctuates along with interest rates; these fluctuating interest rates don't affect the monthly checks from annuities that are already paying income.

Your annuity income will supplement whatever you receive from Social Security. Add in your monthly government check and you might have $1,600 to $2,000 a month, most of which can be spent, because you won't owe a whole lot in income taxes. With any luck, your home will also be paid off by the time you retire, so you can live rent-free. If you are really lucky, you will also have a company pension. But without that pension, you should still be comfortable enough.

Want to do better? Either you have to save a lot more

than $6,000 a year or you have to work longer. Suppose you put off retirement until age seventy. If you salt away $6,000 a year for 20 years, you will have $176,524 at age seventy. If you then sink that entire sum into an immediate-fixed annuity, you might garner monthly income of $1,400 if you are a man and maybe $1,300 if you are a woman. Add your annuity income to Social Security and you are looking at monthly income of between $2,400 and $3,000, some 50 percent higher than the sum you would have had at age sixty-five.

All this points up the power of delaying retirement. It is another way of turning time to your advantage. Why is delaying retirement so powerful? It gives you more time to save and more time to earn investment returns, both of which can mean a much fatter retirement nest egg. But you also shorten your expected time in retirement. That means that you garner a much higher income when you buy an immediate-fixed annuity. It also means that you postpone applying for Social Security, which translates into a bigger monthly check.

I suspect that more and more folks will choose to stay in the work force past age sixty-five, and not just for financial reasons. While many people are anxious to quit the work force, others enjoy the intellectual stimulation of work and they don't relish the prospect of spending 20 or even 30 years in retirement. Still, if you are age fifty and struggling to rebuild your retirement nest egg, I wouldn't assume that you can stay in your current job until age seventy.

Even if you want to keep working, your employer may have other plans. If you are unlucky, you could find yourself pushed into premature retirement in the next round of corporate layoffs. Without a doubt, that would be upsetting. But to make sure that it wouldn't be a financial disaster, you need to build that possibility into your planning. Yes, consider working past age sixty-five. But don't bank on it.

7 GILDING THE GOLDEN YEARS

You made it to retirement. But maybe, like the harried traveler, you didn't quite make it in one piece. There are all kinds of things you forgot, and you will just have to make do with what you have.

Your biggest oversight? Unfortunately, you kept forgetting to save. During those four decades in the work force, there were ample opportunities to sock away money, but again and again they slipped away. So here you are, at age sixty-five, retired and not quite ready. But you will have to make do with what you have.

This chapter is about how to squeeze income out of your retirement savings. It is an endeavor fraught with peril. Think about the risks. You could live longer than you planned for. The stock or bond market might collapse, crushing the value of your mutual funds. You could mismanage your portfolio or end up in the hands of an incompetent or unscrupulous adviser. Inflation might spin out of control. You could get dunned for hefty medical or nursing-home costs.

Make no mistake: Investing in retirement is far more complicated than investing for retirement. When amassing money for your golden years, you save what you can and you try to garner decent investment returns. If you mess up, however, the consequences aren't dire, because your standard of living depends on your paycheck, not your prowess for saving and investing. By contrast, once retired, it really stings when you get it wrong. If you couldn't afford too much financial foolishness during your working years, there is even less room for error now.

Consider, for instance, the issue of how much income to drain off your portfolio each year. Spend too much and you could find yourself in poverty during your waning years. Spend too little and you may look back and realize that you scrimped and saved unnecessarily. You get just one shot at retirement, so it is critical that you settle on the right portfolio-withdrawal rate. Yet, as you will discover, selecting the right rate is no simple matter.

In the years ahead, lots of folks will get their one shot at retirement. The baby boom generation is beginning to retire, and it is not going to be pretty. Newly minted retirees will roll out of the work force, clutching their 401(k) balances. There to greet them will be Wall Street's finest—a motley crew of brokers, financial planners, and mutual-fund companies all anxious to manage their money.

Many retirees will end up with mediocre advice and lackluster returns. A few will be swiftly parted from their money and left to struggle through retirement on Social Security and little else. You can bank on this: In the years ahead, we will be fed a steady diet of newspaper horror stories, each recounting the sad tale of an unwitting retiree who was taken to the cleaners by a crooked investment adviser.

On the other hand, as much as I distrust Wall Street, I also realize that there are plenty of retirees who will need some handholding. You may happily manage your portfolio when you are age sixty-five. But once you are in your eighties, it may all seem a little overwhelming. With that in mind, you might want to line up somebody to help.

Don't think that you will need an investment adviser? Maybe your spouse will, should you die first. If either of you will require financial advice, it is best to find somebody now, before the crisis strikes and your judgment is less sharp. As a starting point, go back and read the section on advisers at the end of Chapter 3.

For now, maybe all you need to do is find a financial planner who takes on hourly work. Spend an hour or two with the financial planner, to get the planner up to speed on your finances and to make sure that you are comfortable with your choice of adviser. Later, if you need additional help, you can always go back and buy more of the adviser's time.

You don't necessarily have to hire a formal adviser. You could always turn to your children for help. Take time now to tell them about your finances and thereafter provide regular updates. If you do that, your kids will be ready to step in, should you need assistance. In fact, even if you use an adviser, briefing your children about your finances is a smart move. That way, they can help out, should you need a second opinion or become incapacitated, and they will be better placed to sort out your affairs after your death.

But maybe the smartest thing you can do is make sensible financial arrangements, setting up a portfolio that is simple, well organized, and easy to manage, thus reducing your need for help. So how can you build a simple portfolio that also generates heaps of income and staves off the many threats mentioned above? That is where we turn next.

WITHDRAWAL SYMPTOMS

Before the recent bear market hit, many financial experts offered retirees a relatively straightforward withdrawal strategy. Don't worry, they counseled, about how much income your portfolio kicks off through dividends and interest. Instead, build a portfolio with maybe 50 percent stocks and 50 percent bonds that will score decent long-run gains through a combination of income and capital gains.

Meanwhile, look to generate income each year by both collecting your dividends and interest and also periodically selling investments. How much could you withdraw each year? Advisers often suggested a 5 percent withdrawal rate. That meant that you would withdraw 5 percent of your portfolio's value in the first year of retirement. In subsequent years, you would step up your annual withdrawals along with inflation.

For instance, if you retired with $400,000, you would withdraw $20,000 in the first year of retirement. Thereafter, if inflation ran at 3 percent a year, you would withdraw $20,600 in your second year of retirement, $21,218 in the third, and so on.

Keep in mind that these sums include any dividends and interest you receive. Let's say that you are supposed to withdraw $20,000 this year. If you collect $9,000 in dividends and interest, then you should only sell $11,000 of investments. Also, bear in mind that not all of this money can be spent. If you are tapping retirement accounts or selling stocks with unrealized gains, part of your annual withdrawal will end up in the taxman's pocket.

Does all this seem reasonable? The strategy of gradually rising withdrawals works wonderfully, provided that you earn returns each year that look like the long-run stock- and bond-market averages. But, of course, the market doesn't work that way. Some years, you get great returns. Some years, performance is dreadful. Short-run results can look nothing like the long-run averages.

This isn't a big deal if you are in the work force and socking away money for the future. But once you are re-tired and living off your portfolio, the sequence of re-turns is critical. During the course of a 20- or 30-year retirement, you will likely face at least one major bear market. With any luck, the bear market will strike late in your retirement, after your nest egg has been fattened by years of healthy gains. What if you are unlucky? The bear market will arrive just as you retire.

Suppose you quit the work force in early 2000. Even if you were well diversified, your stock portfolio might have lost 50 percent. But unlike those still in the work force, your losses were further compounded by your need for spending money. Even as falling share prices eviscerated your portfolio, you were withdrawing money, thereby exacerbating the damage done.

Sure, stock prices will eventually bounce back. But because your portfolio's value has been so reduced by your own withdrawals, you won't fully benefit from the subsequent rebound. The more you withdrew from your stock portfolio during the bear market, the less you will recoup when the bull returns.

What to do? Two lessons are crystal clear: First, you can't blindly increase your withdrawals each year along with inflation, regardless of what is happening to your portfolio's value. Second, when share prices fall sharply, you never want to be in a position where you have to sell stocks to generate spending money. That could be a disaster, because you are locking in your losses and limiting your gains from any subsequent market rebound.

CUSHIONING WITH CASH

As you think about how to manage your money in retirement, a mix of 50 percent stocks and 50 percent conservative investments is a good starting point. A 5 percent withdrawal rate is also a reasonable target. But you will need to tweak these strategies.

As a first step, to protect against market mayhem, I would take the portion of your portfolio that is devoted to conservative investments and put maybe half that money into a short-term corporate-bond fund and a money-market fund. Thus, you would have 25 percent of your overall portfolio in these superconservative investments.

Think of this as your cash cushion. Every year, this is the place you will go to get spending money. With 25 percent of your portfolio invested in your cash cushion, you have enough money there to cover five years' worth of portfolio withdrawals, assuming a 5 percent withdrawal rate.

Meanwhile, take the rest of your portfolio and invest for long-run growth. You might use your portfolio's 50 percent stock allocation to invest in a broad array of stocks, including blue chips, smaller companies, foreign markets, and real-estate investment trusts. What about the conservative portion? You would have 25 percent set aside for your cash cushion and the other 25 percent invested in a mix that might include an inflation-indexed Treasury bond fund, a high-yield junk-bond fund, and a low-cost bond-market index fund.

Put all these various funds together and your portfolio might look like the accompanying pie chart. As you will notice, this portfolio strongly resembles the one I drew up for conservative investors in Chapter 6. There is a good reason for that. Just because you retire doesn't mean that you should radically revamp your investment mix. Even as you siphon off income from your portfolio, you still need to shoot for decent long-run gains, so you offset some of the damage done by inflation.

Every year, aim to replenish your cash reserve by directing all of your mutual-fund income and capital-gains distributions into your short-term corporate-bond fund and your money-market fund. But these distributions alone probably won't be enough to compensate for your annual withdrawals. Instead, each year you will need to sell some stock and bond-fund shares.

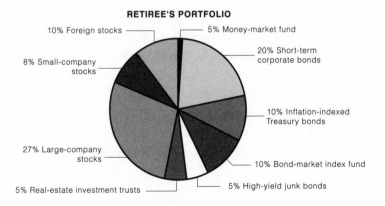

RETIREE'S PORTFOLIO

10% Foreign stocks

5% Money-market fund

20% Short-term corporate bonds

8% Small-company stocks

10% Inflation-indexed Treasury bonds

27% Large-company stocks

10% Bond-market index fund

5% Real-estate investment trusts

5% High-yield junk bonds

In buoyant years for the market, that will be painless enough. Look to sell from across your portfolio, with the goal of both replenishing your cash reserve and getting your portfolio back in line with your target percentages. But in years when either your stocks or your bonds get whacked, I would avoid selling shares of any fund that has been hit hard, even if that means you don't fully replenish your cash cushion.

Have your bonds been crushed? Don't touch them and sell stocks instead. Seen your stock funds tumble? Sell from the bond bucket, while leaving your stocks to rebound. With five years of spending money in your cash reserve, you should be able to sit tight through even a protracted bear market, such as the one that started in 2000, without selling any stock-fund shares.

To give yourself added flexibility when choosing what to sell, favor more specialized funds. While you were in the work force, it was fine to take the path of simplicity, owning as few as three funds (a broad-based U.S.-stock index fund, a foreign-stock index fund, and a single bond fund). But once you retire, you need to spread your money across more specialized funds.

To understand why, imagine blue-chip stocks get hammered next year, but small stocks do just fine. If you own two funds, one that targets small stocks and one that targets blue-chip companies, you can sell some of your small-cap–fund shares, while leaving your blue-chip fund to recover. But if all you own is a single broad-based U.S. stock fund, you don't have any choice. If you sell, you are selling out of all market sectors.

PLAYING THE PERCENTAGES

While a cash cushion will help you to avoid selling stocks at the depth of a bear market, it won't stop you from overspending. If you get returns that look like the long-run stock- and bond-market averages, you should be able to withdraw 5 percent of your portfolio in the first year of retirement and thereafter to step up your withdrawals along with inflation.

But if you are confronted with a punishing bear market, this sort of withdrawal strategy would be suicidal. Even if you aren't forced to sell stocks, your spending will still devastate your portfolio's value and you will eventually be compelled to slash your annual withdrawals.

That reduced income is bad enough. But the decline in your standard of living will be even harsher, once you figure in inflation. True, inflation has been relatively subdued over the past decade, climbing at just 2.9 percent a year in the 1990s. But retirees haven't gotten off as lightly as the rest of the population. Those age sixty-five and over spend a disproportionate amount of their income on medical expenses, especially prescription drugs, and these costs have been climbing at an alarming clip. Combine those rising costs with a shrunken income and you have yourself a vicious inflationary squeeze.

What is the solution? Unfortunately, there isn't one. There is no neat, clean strategy that will ensure that you withdraw the right amount. Instead, you will have to muddle through. My advice: Rather than automatically increasing your annual withdrawals along with inflation, instead aim to make withdrawals each year equal to 5 percent of your portfolio's beginning-of-year value.

This forces you to raise and lower your spending

along with the market. For instance, suppose you retire with $400,000. That first year, you would withdraw 5 percent of that $400,000, equal to $20,000. Let us assume that that first year also turns out to be a good one for the market, and your portfolio finishes the year at $420,000. When calculating your withdrawal for the second year, you would multiply that $420,000 by 5 percent. That would give you $21,000 to spend in the second year. Unfortunately, year two proves to be a rough stretch for the market and your portfolio plunges to $380,000. That means your withdrawal in the third year would be limited to 5 percent of that sum, or $19,000.

If you withdraw 5 percent of your portfolio's value every year, you will never run out of money, because you are always withdrawing a fixed percentage of whatever remains. But this fixed-percentage strategy isn't a panacea. You may end up doing a lot of unnecessary penny-pinching.

Suppose that your portfolio grows over time, even after figuring in your annual withdrawals. That might seem like cause for celebration, because it means that you can drain off a rising stream of income, as you snag your 5 percent cut each year. But your portfolio's rising value also means that you are likely to leave a truckload of money to your ungrateful and undeserving heirs. That is money you could have enjoyed.

As a compromise, I would start with the fixed-percentage strategy and then play it by ear. If you get to your early seventies and your portfolio is growing by leaps and bounds, you might splurge a little, pulling out more than 5 percent in some years. Got a hankering to travel the world or take a ritzy cruise? Take the trip now, before you lose your taste for adventure.

Financial planners often talk about three phases of retirement: the go-go years, the slow-go years, and the no-go years. In the early go-go years, retirees tend to travel extensively and take on expensive new hobbies. If the market dictates that you have to scrimp, then scrimp. But if the market is generous, I would seize the chance to enjoy these years, even if you spend somewhat more than 5 percent of your portfolio's beginning-of-year balance.

In any case, your living expenses will likely decline during the slow-go period. In this phase of retirement, you may find that you spend less than 5 percent a year. What about the no-go period? Your spending could leap again, as you face a sharp rise in medical expenses. You may even find yourself paying for a nursing home. At that point, having a bloated portfolio could come in handy.

You might have reached this point in the chapter with worry gnawing at the pit of your stomach. "Only 5 percent? How will I cope in retirement if I can spend just 5 percent each year?" Many folks are surprised by how little income they can squeeze out of a retirement portfolio. Indeed, unethical financial advisers do a brisk business by promising to generate far larger amounts of income. They can, of course, manage this feat for a few years, but eventually inflation and the market will take their toll, and their clients are left to suffer the consequences.

If you look at your portfolio and find that 5 percent just isn't going to cut it, you have a few options. You

TAKING CARE

Coping with the costs of long-term care is a little beyond the scope of this book. But it is something you clearly need to think about. Medicare doesn't cover nursing-home costs, except for the brief period that might be needed after hospitalization. Medicaid will cover long-term–care costs, but only for those who are impoverished.

How will you cope if you suddenly find yourself paying $60,000 a year for a nursing home? What if both you and your spouse end up needing care, so that the combined tab is $120,000 a year? Insurance companies are currently applying the full-court press, trying to persuade those age fifty and up to buy long-term–care insurance. The problem is, these policies are hugely expensive. Moreover, even if you dig deep and buy a policy, there is no guarantee that your annual premiums won't jump even further in the years ahead.

Nonetheless, you may need long-term–care insurance. But before purchasing a policy, think about how else you might pay for a nursing home or for at-home care. You could cover part of the costs with your monthly Social Security check. You might also be able to cover a portion of the cost with investment and annuity income and with any pension you receive. Tote up your income from all these sources and see what the gap is between your total income and the likely cost of a nursing home. You could then purchase a policy that will pay enough to cover this shortfall.

You should also think carefully about what sort of policy to buy. You can purchase policies where you don't receive benefits until 180 days or a year after you are deemed in need of nursing-home care. Thus, you would have to pay for that initial period out of your own pocket. That might seem rough. But as with a high deductible on an auto-insurance policy, opting for this long waiting period can significantly reduce the cost of a long-term–care policy.

Similarly, you can purchase a policy that pays benefits for just three or five years, or you could buy one that pays benefits for life. Most people will do just fine with a policy with five years' worth of benefits. The typical nursing-home stay is around a year, and very few people stay longer than five years.

Who ends up needing nursing-home care for more than five years? This small minority seems to be comprised largely of folks who suffer from some form of dementia. Worried about that risk? If your family health history is rife with dementia, especially Alzheimer's, you may want to opt for a long-term–care policy with lifetime benefits.

could buy an immediate annuity or take out a reverse mortgage. I will discuss both strategies in a moment. But also consider working part-time. When people quit the work force, most want to quit completely, delighted at the prospect of never working another day in their life. Retirement doesn't seem like retirement if you have to continue working part-time. Still, don't rule it out.

If you can earn $5,000 a year working part-time, that is the equivalent of having another $100,000 in retirement savings. After all, you would need $100,000 to generate that $5,000 in retirement income. Moreover, by working part-time, you may be able to delay Social Security and put off buying an immediate annuity. Result? That delay will work to your advantage, because you will receive bigger monthly checks once you sign on for Social Security and purchase your annuity.

BUYING INCOME

With your cash cushion and your fixed-percentage strategy, you have two tools that will help you cope with bear markets. But bear markets aren't the only risk you face. What if you mismanage your portfolio, through either your own incompetence or bad advice? What if you get lousy long-run returns and it looks like you might outlive your savings? What if a 5 percent withdrawal strategy doesn't generate enough income?

One solution is to invest a chunk of your portfolio in an immediate-fixed annuity. You might take the 25 percent of your portfolio earmarked for inflation-indexed bonds, junk bonds, and a bond-index fund and put some or all of that money into one of these annuities. What will you get for your money? Immediate-fixed annuities can come with all kinds of bells and whistles.

But with the plain-vanilla version, you invest a wad of money, in return for which you get a check every month for the rest of your life, no matter how long you live. The checks you receive will be greater than the interest you could earn by buying high-quality bonds. Those bigger checks, however, come at a price: Usually, when you buy an immediate annuity, the money invested is gone forever.

Because of that feature, many retirees have a visceral reaction against immediate annuities. They hate the idea of investing such a large chunk of cash, knowing that they won't ever see the money again. Partly, it is the old prohibition that you should "never spend your principal" and "never dip into capital." With an immediate-fixed annuity, you aren't just dipping into capital. You are vaporizing it.

But for many retirees, the concern is also more basic than that. What if you buy an immediate annuity and then drop dead the next year? You would have made an extraordinarily bad bet. For that reason, you shouldn't buy an immediate annuity unless you are confident you will live until at least your early eighties. On average, you are likely to live that long. But the averages disguise a huge spread. For proof, consider some numbers from Seattle insurer Safeco Corp.

Safeco took the life expectancy for sixty-five–year-olds and threw out the 15 percent who die the most quickly and the 15 percent who live the longest, leaving only the middle 70 percent. What was the life expectancy for this middle 70 percent? If you are a sixty-five-year-old man, you might live until age seventy-four or you might survive to age ninety-four. Similarly, if you are a sixty-five-year-old woman and you fall into this middle 70 percent, you might die as soon as age seventy-seven or you might live to age ninety-six.

The implication: Even if you assume that you will neither die quickly nor be among those who live the longest, you still have no real sense of your likely life expectancy. Your retirement might last just one decade or it might last three.

But which will it be? If you are going to make intelligent decisions about how to manage your money in retirement, you need to get a better handle on your life expectancy. To that end, try playing with one of the life-expectancy calculators available on the Internet. My favorite can be found at www.livingto100.com.

Likely to live into your eighties? I would seriously consider purchasing an annuity. But what about the risk of an early death? To overcome such concerns, the insurance industry offers policies with a variety of wrinkles. For instance, when you buy an annuity, you can ask for payments to be guaranteed for a minimum of, say, 10 years. That way, if you die earlier than expected, your heirs are guaranteed to get at least some money back. But you will pay a price for such guarantees, in the form of lower monthly income.

Shopping for a fixed annuity is a breeze. First, figure out what sort of policy you want and how much you are willing to invest. Next, contact a bunch of insurers and ask how much monthly income they would pay on the annuity you want. Inclined to purchase the highest-paying annuity? Before you plunk down any money, make sure that the insurer has a top rating for financial strength. You want to be confident the insurance company will still be around in 20 or 30 years to keep sending you those monthly checks.

You can get a slew of annuity quotes by going to Web sites such as www.annuity.com, www.annuityscout. com, and www.immediateannuity.com. But you might also go directly to well-known, top-rated insurers, such as Berkshire Hathaway (www.brkdirect.com), TIAA–CREF (www.tiaa-cref.org), and USAA (www.usaa.com). Meanwhile, if you want to get a handle on an insurance company's rating for financial strength, check with one of the credit-rating agencies. You can find a list of their Web sites in the appendix at the back of this book.

If immediate-fixed annuities are such a great investment, why not pour your entire savings into one of these things? Immediate-fixed annuities have one huge drawback. And, no, the drawback isn't that your investment disappears with your death and thus there will be nothing left for your heirs. Frankly, that is a qualm that many retirees can't afford, especially after the recent stock-market collapse. Rather, the problem is that immediate-fixed annuities leave you vulnerable to inflation. Your monthly checks will stay the same, while inflation marches relentlessly on.

In any given year, the impact of rising consumer prices will be modest. But over time, it can have a devastating effect. Remember how indexing and holding down costs can snowball? Inflation works the same way, but the end result is far less pleasant. At 3 percent inflation per year, the spending power of your annuity checks will be cut in half after 23 years. That is why I suggest limiting a fixed annuity to 25 percent of your portfolio, while continuing to hold other investments that will generate long-run growth.

If you put 25 percent of your portfolio in an immediate annuity and you find that the resulting income covers a hefty portion of your annual spending needs, you might settle for a slightly smaller cash reserve. That will allow you to use part of your cash-cushion money to shoot for higher long-run returns, by investing more in high-yield junk bonds, inflation-indexed Treasury bonds, or your bond-market index fund.

Tempted to put even more in an immediate annuity? If you are really strapped for cash and trying to squeeze maximum income out of your savings, that might make sense. But rather than buying a regular immediate-fixed annuity, consider two alternatives.

Some insurers, including American Express's IDS Life Insurance Co., Canada Life Financial Corp., Lincoln National Corp., and Safeco, sell immediate-fixed annuities where the payment is stepped up by a fixed percentage each year. You might opt for an annuity where your monthly check rises by 3 or 4 percent annually, which will help blunt the damage done by inflation. In return for getting that growing stream of income, you have to accept a lower initial monthly income. Still, given the threat from inflation, these rising-income annuities seem like a prudent choice, especially if you are going to invest the bulk of your nest egg in an annuity.

What is the other alternative? It is a maddeningly complicated product known as an immediate-variable annuity. You might be aware of its more popular cousin, the tax-deferred variable annuity. With a tax-deferred variable annuity, you can save for retirement by investing in a menu of stock, bond, and money-market mutual funds held within the annuity.

An immediate-variable annuity has a similar structure, but the goal is to generate retirement income. You invest a lump sum in a collection of mutual funds. Thereafter, your monthly income depends on how those funds perform. If your funds outperform a hurdle rate, normally set at 3 to 7 percent a year, your monthly checks will rise, thus allowing you to keep up with inflation.

But what if you fail to beat the hurdle rate? Your checks will shrivel. For instance, if you stick your immediate-variable annuity money in stock funds and the market implodes, your monthly income will shrink sharply. Clearly, an immediate-variable annuity can be a far riskier animal than an immediate-fixed annuity.

There are other problems with immediate-variable annuities. Not only are these things inordinately expensive, but it is also mighty tough to figure out which product is the best deal. Many companies don't offer the same hurdle rates, so it is difficult to compare one promised income stream with another. But even if you find two products with the same hurdle rate, you still can't make a clean comparison.

Instead, you have to weigh the size of the initial monthly check against the immediate-variable annuity's total annual expenses. The higher those expenses, the harder it will be to earn decent long-run returns. Should you pick the immediate-variable annuity with the biggest initial check but hefty annual expenses, or should you go for the smaller check from the annuity with lower expenses? Let's face it, this stuff is enough to make your head spin.

Fortunately, in the end, it turns out to be an easy choice. As of this writing, there is just one stand-alone immediate-variable annuity with reasonable costs, and that is offered by TIAA–CREF. It is the only immediate-variable annuity that I would consider buying.

Don't like TIAA–CREF's product? If you are really intrigued by immediate-variable annuities, there is one other option that is worth exploring. If you find a low-cost tax-deferred variable annuity that you like, you could purchase that product and then, after a brief waiting period, convert it to an immediate-variable annuity. But before going that route, check out all the details, including costs, hurdle rates and your likely initial monthly income.

PUTTING IT ON THE HOUSE

Earlier, I noted that people often describe their home as their best investment, largely because it forces them to save. But for most folks, the only return from their house turns out to be the ability to live rent-free. Want to squeeze even more out of your home? Once retired, seriously consider trading down to a smaller, more manageable place. That will allow you to cut property taxes, maintenance costs, utility bills, and the annual premium on your homeowner's insurance. With any luck, you will also free up some home equity, which you can then spend.

Trading down will mean paying a fistful of costs to sell your current place and buy a new one. Because the tab is so steep, be sure that you pick your new home carefully, preferably selecting a location that is close to stores, restaurants, public transportation, and other amenities. You don't want to have to move again, incurring another costly round of moving expenses.

Thinking of relocating to another part of the country? If you are wondering where to move, check out www.bestplaces.net, especially its tool that can help you identify a suitable location to live based on the criteria you deem most important.

Trading down is one way to unlock some of your home's equity. Need even more money? After you have traded down, or as an alternative to moving, you could take out a reverse mortgage. These loans allow you to tap into the value of your home without actually selling your residence.

Many retirees don't like the idea of a reverse mortgage because, like an immediate annuity, it smacks of dipping into capital. Still, while hardly a financial best-seller, reverse mortgages are becoming increasingly popular. According to the U.S. Department of Housing and Urban Development, lenders closed on a record 13,049 federally insured reverse mortgages during the fiscal year ending September 2002. That was a 63 percent increase over the previous record, set in 1999.

Reverse mortgages can be an expensive proposition. But the costs involved shouldn't be too steep, as long as you stick with a home equity conversion mortgage. HECM reverse mortgages are insured by the Federal Housing Administration. The cash from a reverse mortgage can be received in three ways: You can ask for a lump sum, have the equity in your home available via a credit line, or arrange to get a monthly check, comparable to what you receive from an immediate-fixed annuity.

Indeed, you could find yourself collecting two checks each month: one from your annuity and one from your reverse mortgage. Provided you don't move or sell your home, the money received from a reverse mortgage doesn't have to be repaid until the last owner of the house dies. At that point, the amount owed cannot exceed your home's value.

Intrigued? To find out more, call AARP at 1-800-424-3410 and ask for its pamphlet on reverse mortgages. That pamphlet is also available online at www.aarp.org/revmort. In addition, AARP has a calculator online that will help you figure out how much cash you might receive from a reverse mortgage. To go directly to the calculator, direct your browser to www.rmaarp.com.

CALLING ON UNCLE SAM

Many retirees apply for Social Security retirement benefits as soon as they quit the work force. They need the cash, so they don't have much choice. But even seniors with great financial flexibility often apply right away. After decades of contributing to Social Security, many retirees are anxious to get a little bit of their money back, so they start their monthly check the moment they quit working.

But this haste may prove costly in the long run. Retirees can take Social Security as early as age sixty-two or they can wait until age seventy. If you are still working, it almost never makes sense to apply for Social Security early, because your benefits will probably end up being taxed and they could be eliminated entirely.

Suppose, however, that you retire fully at age sixty-two. Should you apply for Social Security right away or should you delay? There is no one right answer. But it is worth giving the decision careful thought, rather than automatically opting for benefits as soon as you retire.

Social Security will give you a check every month, just like an immediate annuity and a reverse mortgage (assuming you choose to receive your reverse mortgage as a monthly check). But Social Security is a far more desirable source of retirement income. Your monthly check is guaranteed by the government, it rises each year along with inflation, it is at least partially tax-free, and you will get this income every month for as long as you live. Given all those benefits, wouldn't you want to get as much of this income as possible? The longer you delay Social Security, the bigger your monthly check will be.

Take people born between 1943 and 1954. For this group, the full retirement age is sixty-six. But these folks can claim Social Security as early as age sixty-two and receive a monthly check that is 25 percent smaller. Alternatively, they could hold out until age seventy and get a check that is 32 percent bigger.

In other words, if you are eligible for $1,000 a month at age sixty-six, you could receive $750 at age sixty-two or hold out for $1,320 at age seventy. But which is the best option? As with an immediate annuity, it depends partly on how long you think you will live. But you are also making a bet on what sort of investment returns you expect to earn.

If you apply for Social Security early, that means that you won't have to withdraw quite so much from your portfolio in the early years of retirement. That can be a smart move if you are optimistic about your portfolio and expect to earn handsome investment returns. On the other hand, if you are optimistic about your life expectancy, you would want to delay Social Security and hold out for the larger monthly check.

How does this all shake out? Let's assume you earn middling investment returns. In that case, if you live until at least age eighty-three, you will usually be better off postponing Social Security until age sixty-six, so that you get full retirement benefits. But if you don't think you will live that long, you should probably claim your benefit as soon as you are eligible.

For some seniors, the decision will be easy. They will apply for Social Security right away, because they need the money or because their own health or their family health history is poor. But for most retirees, it will be a tough call. There is a good reason for that. Uncle Sam isn't stupid. The system is designed so that somebody with a typical life expectancy should be indifferent between taking the smaller check at age sixty-two or sixty-three and the large check at age sixty-six or sixty-eight.

Men should be more inclined to apply early, because their life expectancy is shorter than women's, while women should be tempted to delay because of their longer life expectancy. But even men with only a so-so life expectancy may want to delay. By delaying, a husband can ensure that his wife receives a larger survivor's benefit, assuming that he dies first and that he was the family's principal breadwinner.

Still on the fence? Don't necessarily trust your financial adviser on this one. Financial advisers have an incentive to push clients to apply early. If you take Social Security early, you will run down your portfolio more slowly during your initial retirement years. That means that your adviser will have more money to manage and thus will likely earn more income off your account.

My recommendation: If you are undecided after weighing the above arguments, consider delaying benefits, for a couple of reasons. First, as I mentioned earlier, one of the biggest risks in retirement is longevity risk. Even if you outlive your other savings, you know that your government check will keep arriving every month. If you are in your early nineties and your portfolio is rapidly giving out, getting that bigger check could make a huge difference. Throw in your monthly income from an immediate-fixed annuity and a reverse mortgage and you will have a decent safety net in place, should you beat the actuarial tables.

Second, there is the risk of lousy investment returns. Maybe the stock market will generate dreadful results. Maybe you will make foolish investment mistakes. Maybe you will fall into the hands of an incompetent or unethical adviser, who trades your portfolio into the ground. Delaying Social Security, so you get the bigger check, provides useful insurance against these disasters.

Moreover, even if your portfolio performs just fine, that regular income can be enormously comforting. As you grow older, overseeing your stocks and bonds may start to seem like a struggle. But you don't need any fancy money-management skills to cash your three monthly checks: one from your annuity, one from your reverse mortgage, and one from Uncle Sam.

MAKING RETIREMENT LESS TAXING

If you hold down your spending, you can make your retirement nest egg last longer. Any costs that are ripe for cutting? We have already talked about trading down, so you reduce your housing costs. But also check out your 1040. In all likelihood, your annual tax bill is one of your biggest expenses.

If you have been at all diligent in saving for retirement and at all successful at investing, you will reach age sixty-five with investment accounts that have huge embedded tax bills. Much or all of your retirement-account withdrawals will be taxable as ordinary income. Similarly, in your taxable account, you may hold stocks and stock funds with hefty unrealized capital gains.

If you can figure out a way to pay less of this money in taxes, you will have more for yourself. On that score, retirement offers an array of intriguing possibilities. The greatest opportunities occur in your sixties. By age seventy, you have to start collecting Social Security, which will increase your taxable income. Similarly, starting at age $70\frac{1}{2}$, you have to begin withdrawing a minimum sum each year from your retirement accounts. That will also drive up your taxable income, leaving you with less room to manipulate your tax bill.

But before you start receiving Social Security and before you begin making required minimum distributions from your retirement accounts, you will have heaps of room to maneuver. Think about it. You don't have a paycheck anymore. The only income you are receiving is the gains kicked off by the stocks, bonds, and mutual funds held in your taxable account. It is entirely possible, once you figure in the standard deduction and the exemption allowed for yourself and your spouse, that you will owe nothing in taxes.

Sound good? Actually, it isn't. If your income is that low and you expect to be taxed at 27 percent or above later in retirement, you should try to generate a certain amount of gains, so you take full advantage of your current low tax bracket. I would look to realize enough capital gains and generate enough income each year to get yourself to the top of the 15 percent federal income-tax bracket, but no higher.

What does that mean in practice? If you are single, you could earn as much as $36,200 in 2003 and still be in the 15 percent income-tax bracket. Are you age sixty-five or older? Add on another $1,150. Meanwhile, if you are married filing jointly, you can earn as much as $61,500 and remain within the 15 percent bracket. If you are age sixty-five or older, this figure will be $950 higher. If your spouse is also sixty-five or older, tack on an additional $950. These figures assume that you take the standard deduction and one personal exemption each. If a new tax law is passed in 2003, the thresholds for staying within the 15 percent tax bracket could be somewhat higher.

Deliberately realizing extra taxable income each year might seem idiotic. But there is a method to this madness. Paying tax at 15 percent now may be painful. But if you don't realize the gains now, you will likely have to realize those gains later, at which point you may be in a much higher tax bracket. Indeed, many retirees end up getting taxed at surprisingly steep rates once they turn age 70½ and are forced to start drawing down their retirement accounts.

How should you go about boosting your taxable income early in retirement? The easiest strategy is to withdraw money from your retirement accounts. As a rule, you want to delay your retirement-account withdrawals for as long as possible, so that you continue to get that tax-deferred growth. But if you find yourself in the 15 percent tax bracket and expect to be in a higher tax bracket later, go ahead and take the tax hit. If you don't need the spending money, you can simply reinvest your retirement-account withdrawals in your taxable account.

Better still, you could convert part or all of your individual retirement account to a Roth IRA. You can make a conversion only if your income during the year is under $100,000. The sum converted doesn't count toward the $100,000 limit. You will have to pay income taxes on the taxable amount converted. Nonetheless, that can be a smart strategy. Once the money is in a Roth IRA, it will grow tax-free. Moreover, money in a Roth isn't governed by the minimum distribution rules that apply to regular IRAs.

You could also increase your taxable income by revamping your taxable account. Consider selling stocks that have big unrealized gains and look to bolster your annual income by overhauling your bond portfolio. During your working years, when you bought bonds for your taxable account, you might have favored tax-free municipals. But now that you are retired, it may make sense to dump your munis and buy higher-yielding taxable bonds. Even after paying Uncle Sam his due, you will likely be better off with taxable bonds, thanks to your new lower tax bracket.

Similarly, during your working years, you might have purchased savings bonds, because you wanted your interest to grow tax-deferred. Once you quit the work force, consider selling those bonds and paying the necessary tax, thereby taking advantage of your lower tax bracket.

8 SAVING YOURSELF

I hate the word *empowerment*. It is one of those appalling pieces of jargon that is sure to make the skin crawl. It ranks right up there with other notable linguistic abominations, including companies that "grow" their earnings despite being "impacted" by the recession.

Still, I can't deny it. This book is about empowerment. It is about giving hope to investors who were impacted by the stock-market decline and who need to grow their portfolios. It is about how to save yourself, so that you can retire on time and in comfort. But how are you going to save yourself? This book offers six key lessons:

- Focus on the little things. Hold down taxes. Cut investment costs. Favor index funds. Rebalance regularly. Save a little more each month. In any given year, these strategies will only marginally improve your portfolio's performance. But over time, they will snowball into significant wealth.

- If you want to be confident of salvaging your retirement, don't bet everything on stocks, or bonds, or real estate. There is no one right investment. Instead, to garner decent gains without risking disaster, you need to buy a little bit of everything.

■ Stocks are likely to post modest gains in the decade ahead, with a globally diversified portfolio delivering maybe 8 percent a year. With returns so low, the temptation is to shoot for market-beating performance. But you would be smarter to focus on capturing as much of the market's return as possible, by building a globally diversified portfolio of low-cost index funds.

■ To complement your stock portfolio, aim to lock up a healthy stream of income by adding investments such as real-estate investment trusts, high-yield junk bonds, inflation-indexed Treasury bonds, and high-quality corporate bonds. These income-generating investments, which are best held in tax-sheltered retirement accounts, shouldn't fare too much worse than stocks over the decade ahead. In fact, REITs and junk bonds have a decent shot at outperforming stocks.

■ Because the performance gap between stocks and other investments probably won't be that wide, you may reap a handsome rebalancing bonus. To collect that bonus, you need to set target percentages for your various portfolio holdings and then rebalance regularly to bring your investment mix back into line with these targets.

■ If you want to amass enough by age sixty-five and have sufficient income in retirement, you will need to sacrifice. That doesn't just mean saving more each month. You should also think carefully about how much you can afford to spend on other goals. You would no doubt love to bequeath your home and your investment portfolio to your heirs. But to ensure a comfortable retirement, you may need to deplete these assets by annuitizing a big chunk of your investment portfolio and by taking out a reverse mortgage.

What do these six lessons have in common? None of the strategies advocated involves the dubious pursuit of market-beating returns. I am not telling you to bet on star fund managers, trade like a dervish, bank everything on the next hot sector, or hitch your fortunes to some market-timing guru. Many investors tried that nonsense in the 1990s, with decidedly mixed results. Instead, the goal here is the sensible pursuit of wealth by doing everything possible to stack the odds in your favor.

Of course, I could be wrong about the stock market's performance in the decade ahead. The market is the great humbler and I am fully prepared to be humiliated. Maybe stocks will surprise me and post healthy double-digit returns over the next 10 years. In all likelihood, there will be one or two years of spectacular returns, when the Standard & Poor's 500-stock index climbs 25 or even 30 percent. Indeed, when the next bull market kicks in, I wouldn't be surprised to see a brief stretch of dazzling gains.

But even if I am wrong about the S&P 500's performance, it still makes sense to behave as though returns will be modest. Holding down investment costs, trimming taxes, indexing, diversifying, and rebalancing are all smart strategies, no matter what the market's direction.

Moreover, if you assume low returns, you will feel compelled to save diligently. That will put you on track to retire in comfort, whether stocks post great returns or modest results. By contrast, if you bank on double-digit annual gains, you will likely save relatively little. What if the stock market then disappoints? You could find yourself in a heap of trouble.

SUMMONING THE COURAGE

If this book makes investing seem simple, there is a good reason for that. Investing is simple. To be sure, you can make it ludicrously complicated. But when it is complicated, that is usually a sign that Wall Street is raking in fat fees and some poor sucker is headed for the shearing shed. Options? Futures? Mortgage derivatives? Hedge funds? Ignore that garbage.

While sensible investing may be simple, that doesn't mean that it is easy. There is a reason brokers and financial planners continue to thrive. These folks may not have any great insight into which way the stock market is headed or what will happen to interest rates. After reading this book, you probably know as much about investing as the vast majority of brokers and planners.

So why do advisers exist? They encourage their clients to save. They push investors to get money out of savings accounts and into higher-returning investments. They stop customers from panicking during market declines. They provide the emotional fortitude that some investors can't summon on their own.

Clearly, there are folks who need this emotional crutch. Clearly, some people are incapable of making wise investment decisions on their own. Clearly, if you can't bring yourself to straighten out your portfolio and to invest wisely, you should seek the help of an experienced, ethical, low-cost adviser. Do you need help? For an answer, look no further than your behavior over the past three years. If the bear market took an unbearable emotional toll, I would seriously consider hiring an adviser.

But I think that most investors are capable of going it alone. The challenge isn't figuring out what to do. That is fairly easy. Instead, the real challenge is getting yourself to do it. Fixing a bonehead portfolio can be agonizing. Battered by huge stock-market losses, we find it hard to muster the confidence needed to act. We hate to sell at a loss. We don't want to make big changes for fear of compounding our earlier errors.

But if you can find the necessary courage, the benefits are enormous. It is not just that you will put yourself on the path to a comfortable retirement and that you will save yourself a truckload of investment-advisory fees. Rather, the benefit lies in a sense of financial freedom. You won't become wealthy overnight. But you will have control of your financial life. Instead of a gnawing sense of uncertainty, you will know what you own, why you own it, and what it will take to get from here to retirement.

How do you prod yourself into action? In Chapter 6, I encouraged you to sketch out crucial details of your financial plan and then post them on the refrigerator. That is a great place to start. Write down how much money you will save each month. Decide when you will rebalance. List which funds you will buy and what percentage of your portfolio you will invest in each. Finding it tough to decide what mix of funds to buy? Try narrowing the choice. Settle on a single no-load, low-cost fund family and then pick exclusively from among that company's funds.

Next, draw up a timetable for moving money out of your current investments and into your target portfolio. If you own a slew of battered stocks and mutual funds, it can be tough to abandon your losers all at once. Instead, take your time, moving from your current investments to your new portfolio over the course of a year or 18 months. But whatever you do, take that first step. From there, it only gets easier.

STAYING THE COURSE

Once you have rebuilt your portfolio, you have to find some way to stick with your new, better-diversified investment mix. In many ways, this book is an ode to diversification. But I readily concede that diversification has its limits.

Yes, it reduces risk, by ensuring that your portfolio won't get badly bloodied by a single rotten stock or a long-suffering market sector. But there is a limit to the psychological solace that diversification offers. In theory, we should each construct a well-diversified portfolio and then focus on the entire portfolio's results. In practice, we tend to fret about each investment we own.

Despite this drawback, you should still build a globally diversified portfolio that includes stocks, bonds, and real estate. But try to package your portfolio in a way that you find most appealing. I like owning specialized funds, because there always seems to be at least one fund that is performing well and I can take comfort in that fund's performance. Moreover, with specialized funds, there are greater opportunities to rebalance and more choice when it comes time to sell funds to generate retirement income.

But there is a downside to this portfolio of specialized funds. Even as some funds sparkle, others will be sinking. That carnage can be unnerving. Find all that turmoil difficult to stomach? First, make a point of tracking your entire portfolio's value, thereby counteracting the tendency to lose sleep over each fund's performance. Second, if you are an antsy investor, skip specialized stock-index funds and instead stick with diversified funds. These diversified funds will tend to perform more sedately.

No matter how you design your portfolio, however, you will have your rough moments. How do you keep yourself calm through the inevitable market turmoil? The key, I believe, is making sure that there is a good match between your expectations and your investments. Why do some people panic when their investments lose value? Often, their investments aren't behaving in an unusual manner. Rather, the problem lies with investors themselves. They incorrectly expected low risk and got scared when reality hit.

If you want to ensure that your expectations are in line with your investments, try this trick: Mentally divide your portfolio into two accounts: "safe money" and "growth money." Your safe-money account is designed to keep you from being poor. Your growth-money account is designed to make you rich.

Your growth money should include your stocks, real-estate investment trusts, and high-yield junk bonds. With this money, you should be fully prepared for a rough ride, with occasional bear-market losses of 30 or 40 percent or even more. But in return for that rougher ride, you ought to earn healthy returns over time.

Meanwhile, your safe money should consist of your short-term bond fund, bond-market index fund, money-market fund, inflation-indexed Treasury bonds, and other conservative investments. At a minimum, this pool of money ought to include any money you will need to spend within the next five years.

But your safe-money account should also be big enough to make you feel safe. This is the portion of your portfolio that shouldn't generate any unpleasant surprises. Unnerved by your growth account's performance? You should be able to look at the size of your safe-money account and feel reassured.

ENJOYING THE SHOW

The advice in this book will help you to retire on time and with a decent standard of living. But I fully realize that buying index funds isn't nearly as much fun as betting on hot tips and high-flying stocks. Do you miss the wild, lucrative days of the late 1990s? As I noted in Chapter 2, we are the enemy. Investing is about so much more than making money. It is, unfortunately, a chaotic, unnerving, exhilarating maelstrom of greed and fear.

We talk about our stock-market earnings. But we don't earn anything. Companies earn money, which propels their share prices higher. As investors, we just go along for the ride. The market returns what it does and we just divvy up the rewards. But this business of investing doesn't seem like a simple matter of dividing the spoils.

I often describe Wall Street as America's most vibrant entertainment business. Never was that truer than in the late 1990s. Then, many people got hooked on investing. The subsequent market collapse may have driven away the faint of heart. But for us investment junkies, the market remains utterly compelling. We enjoy following our investments. We get a kick out of trading. We like talking about our portfolios. We want that emotional attachment, that sense of involvement with our money, that feeling that we are part of a larger community.

This, I believe, is one reason we try to beat the market. It heightens our sense of excitement and our sense of involvement. When we buy stocks and actively managed mutual funds and we invariably end up with lackluster performance, maybe it isn't a total loss. Maybe, in fact, we are getting good value for our money. Like the moviegoers who cough up $8.50 at the box office, maybe we happily pay a price in investment performance for the thrill of being part of it all.

After the market losses of the past few years, you probably can't afford to indulge too heavily in the beat-the-market fantasy. Find it hard to restrain yourself? Go ahead and indulge a little, by adding a third layer to your portfolio.

In addition to growth money and safe money, you may also want to include some "fun money." This should be no more than 5 percent of your portfolio and preferably less than 3 percent. Think of your fun-money account as your emotional safety valve. With this money, you can do all the crazy things that you used to do in the 1990s.

Heard a hot tip? Got some hunch about the market's direction? Use your fun money to make these bets. Trade like crazy. Dabble in sector funds. Bet on individual stocks. And for goodness sake, enjoy yourself. After all, you will probably end up with a bunch of investment losses, so you might as well get your money's worth.

But with any luck, you will eventually decide that you don't need a fun-money account. I consider it unnecessary. It is possible to reap enormous pleasure from your portfolio without aiming to beat the market. Wall Street really is America's most vibrant entertainment business. But you don't need a ticket to enjoy the show.

Since my childhood in Washington, D.C., I have followed the Baltimore Orioles and the Washington Redskins. Even today, I look for their scores in the paper. If either team is playing and the game is on television, I might watch for half an hour. What if the team loses? It is no big deal. There is always next season.

You should take the same attitude toward the market. By all means follow the daily action. Enjoy the craziness. Read about the cast of characters, the gurus who come and go, the fund managers who hit the top of the performance charts and then nosedive into ignominy, the Masters of the Universe who turn out to be little better than petty thieves. Investing is a wonderful spectator sport. What if your funds lose money this year? There is always next season. If you own a sensible, well-diversified, low-cost portfolio, your time will come.

When the market tumbles, investment advisers sometimes suggest leaving your mutual-fund statements unopened and not bothering to check your brokerage-account balance. Ignore the current turmoil, advise the experts. Behave like a long-term investor, they counsel. In my *Wall Street Journal* columns, I have given the same advice. But maybe this is unrealistic.

Maybe a better tactic is to immerse yourself in investing. Read some of the fine books on investing, like those by Peter Bernstein, William Bernstein, John Bogle, Charles Ellis, Burton Malkiel, and Jeremy Siegel. Occasionally, pick up a copy of *BusinessWeek, Forbes, Fortune, Kiplinger's, Money,* or *Smart Money.* Scour *The Wall Street Journal* or the business section of your local paper. Watch CNBC.

And enjoy it all, with that sense of detachment that comes with knowledge. Everybody else is trying to pick the winners. You know that most of them will end up losing. They are worried about today's market action. You are focused on the next decade. They are ebullient one moment, crushed the next. You have the quiet confidence that comes with a well–thought-out investment plan.

CONTROLLING YOUR FUTURE

When you divvy up your portfolio between safe money, growth money, and fun money, you aren't just organizing your portfolio. You are also taking a key step toward controlling your emotions. Control? That, I would argue, is a crucial concept in money management.

In fact, I harked on the notion of control right at the start of Chapter 1. We spend far too much time trying to control the uncontrollable. We try to guess the stock market's direction. We try to pick the next hot stocks. We try to select superstar funds. And more often than not, we fail miserably. We cannot control the market. Trying to pick market-beating investments is a loser's game.

Instead, you should focus on what you can control. You may not be able to pick the next hot fund. But you can make sure that your funds have rock-bottom annual expenses, so that you keep more of whatever you make. You can't predict whether stocks will rise or fall over the next 12 months. But you can control your portfolio's risk level, so that you fare just fine, no matter what happens to stock prices in the year ahead. You can't pick winning stocks. But you can save a healthy sum every month, so that you will have enough for retirement, even if stock and bond performance is disappointing.

The bear market has done its damage. Your challenge is to deal with the fallout. No doubt some folks have abandoned stocks, swearing never to return. No doubt others are scanning the market, looking for hot investments that will somehow miraculously undo the damage done by three years of market turmoil.

But what are you going to do? This, I believe, is a

great time to be investing. But to be confident of making good money in the years ahead, you need to invest prudently. Keep costs low. Make full use of retirement accounts. Save. Diversify. Avoid mental mistakes. This stuff isn't exciting. But investing was never meant to be exciting. It is meant to be profitable. Want to retire in comfort? It is time to save yourself.

APPENDIX: WEB SITES

Dot-com stocks may have been an unmitigated disaster. But the Internet boom wasn't all for naught. The Web has emerged as the intelligent investor's finest resource. Want to implement the strategies discussed in this book? Check out the sites below.

MUTUAL FUNDS

For ordinary investors, the best place to buy index funds and low-cost bond funds is usually Vanguard Group (www.vanguard.com). Other sources include Bridgeway Funds (www.bridgewayfund.com), Dreyfus Corp. (www.dreyfus.com), Fidelity Investments (www.fidelity.com), T. Rowe Price Associates (www.troweprice.com), Charles Schwab Corp. (www.schwab.com), TIAA–CREF (www.tiaa-cref.org), and USAA Investment Management (www.usaa.com).

Index funds are also available from Dimensional Fund Advisors (www.dfafunds.com). But to purchase these funds, you have to go through an investment adviser approved by DFA.

Prefer exchange-traded index funds? Barclays Global Investors (www.ishares.com) offers the broadest array of such funds. To buy exchange-traded funds, you could go through a discount broker. But also check out low-cost Internet stock-purchasing services such as Buyand-Hold (www.buyandhold.com) and ShareBuilder (www.sharebuilder.com).

Meanwhile, to find key details on any fund, visit Morningstar's Web site (www.morningstar.com). While the site includes premium services, for which you have to pay a subscription, much of the information on the site is available at no charge.

BONDS

If you are interested in purchasing either conventional Treasury bonds or inflation-indexed Treasury bonds, consider buying directly from the government through the TreasuryDirect program (www.treasurydirect.gov). What about savings bonds? For more on those, go to www.savingsbonds.gov.

ANNUITIES

If you are retired and looking to buy an immediate-fixed annuity, get a bunch of quotes by going to www.annuity.com, www.annuityscout.com, and www.immediateannuity.com. Also, check out well-regarded providers of immediate annuities such as Berkshire Hathaway (www.brkdirect.com), TIAA–CREF (www.tiaa-cref.org), and USAA Life Insurance Co. (www.usaa.

com). TIAA–CREF offers both immediate-fixed annuities and a low-cost immediate-variable annuity.

Meanwhile, if you are saving for retirement, you might be interested in tax-deferred fixed annuities. In that case, consider the offerings from Fidelity (www.fidelity.com), Schwab (www.schwab.com), USAA, and Vanguard (www.vanguard.com). Fidelity and USAA also offer a fixed annuity as one of the investment options within their tax-deferred variable annuities. Similarly, T. Rowe Price (www.troweprice.com) and TIAA–CREF have fixed options in their tax-deferred variable annuities.

How do you know if you have yourself a good deal? For comparison purposes, get yields on a host of tax-deferred fixed annuities by going to www.annuity.com and www.annuityscout.com. As you hunt for the right tax-deferred fixed annuity, be leery of high first-year "teaser" rates and pay careful attention to the surrender charges involved.

Before buying any sort of annuity, check the financial strength of the insurance company involved by going to www.ambest.com, www.fitchratings.com, www.moodys.com, and www.standardandpoors.com. The information on financial strength is free. But be warned: At some of the sites, locating these free ratings can take a little digging.

While the credit-rating agencies all give letter grades to indicate financial strength, they don't all use the same scale. But as a rule of thumb, I wouldn't buy an annuity from any insurer that doesn't have some sort of A rating for financial strength.

REAL ESTATE

To see how much you can save by making extra-principal payments on your mortgage, try playing with the calculators at www.bankrate.com, www.hsh.com, www.mortgage-x.com, and www.realestateabc.com.

Among those, my favorite is the mortgage calculator at www.bankrate.com. Why? Suppose that you have made extra-principal payments in the past, so you are already on track to pay off your mortgage ahead of schedule. Now, you want to pay off another chunk of your loan's balance.

The www.bankrate.com calculator makes it relatively easy to figure out the benefit of those additional payments. First, enter your current loan balance and interest rate and use today's date as the loan's start date. Next, play around with the term of the mortgage, until the monthly mortgage payment shown matches your current regular monthly principal-and-interest payment. Once you have that information correct, you can then analyze the benefit of making further extra-principal payments.

AARP (www.aarp.org/revmort) offers a useful guide to reverse mortgages. While there, try the calculator at www.rmaarp.com, which will give you an idea of how much money you might garner from a reverse mortgage. If you want even more information on reverse mortgages, go to the sites offered by the National Center for Home Equity Conversion (www.reverse.org) and the National Reverse Mortgage Lenders Association (www.reversemortgage.org).

Don't like the idea of a reverse mortgage? To free up home equity and cut your cost of living, maybe instead you want to trade down and possibly even relocate. With that in mind, visit www.bestplaces.net and play with the search tool labeled "find your best place to live."

INVESTMENT ADVISERS

Before you go hunting for an investment adviser, you might want to get some sense for what sort of advisers are out there and how much they charge. To that end, check out the services offered by Evanson Asset Management (www.evansonasset.com), Garrett Planning Network (www.garrettplanningnetwork.com), Portfolio Solutions (www.psinvest.com), and Vanguard (www. vanguard.com). All provide a low-cost way of getting investment advice.

Want to locate a financial planner in your area? Try the Financial Planning Association (www.fpanet.org) or the National Association of Personal Financial Advisors (www.feeonly.org). To be a member of NAPFA, a financial planner is not allowed to accept commissions. Has an adviser qualified to be a certified financial planner? For an answer, go to the Web site offered by the Certified Financial Planner Board of Standards (www.cfp-board.org).

To find out whether a broker or investment adviser is properly licensed or registered and to see whether he or she has a clean regulatory record, begin at the Securities and Exchange Commission (www.sec.gov/investor/brokers.htm). From there, you will be directed to other sites where you can check out potential advisers.

FINANCIAL CALCULATORS

A host of financial-planning calculators are available at www.bankrate.com, www.choosetosave.org, moneycentral. msn.com, and www.quicken.com.

Many fund-company Web sites also offer useful financial-planning tools. Maybe the best collection can be found at the T. Rowe Price site (www.troweprice.com). In particular, check out the site's retirement-income calculator (www3.troweprice.com/ric/RIC), which will give you a sense of how much monthly income you can squeeze out of your retirement savings.

Similarly, you can road test your retirement-spending strategy by going to www.early-retirement.org. The calculator there will show how you would have fared historically, assuming that you retired in 1871, in 1872, in 1873, and so on.

To get a handle on your likely longevity, direct your browser to www.livingto100.com. For a second opinion, try moneycentral.msn.com/investor/calcs/n_expect/main. asp.

Want an estimate of your Social Security retirement benefits? Visit www.ssa.gov/OACT/ANYPIA and use its quick calculator.

KEEPING UP

Morningstar (www.morningstar.com) doesn't just offer a wealth of information. You may also enjoy the Web site's Vanguard Diehards bulletin board, which is the online meeting place for Bogleheads, investors inspired by

Vanguard Group founder John Bogle. Puzzled by some aspect of investing? The Diehards bulletin board is a great place to pose your question.

Index-fund aficionados might also visit IndexFunds (www.indexfunds.com), which contains good information on both regular index funds and exchange-traded index funds, and Efficient Frontier (www.efficientfrontier.com), a quarterly digest devoted to key investment issues. Efficient Frontier is edited by William Bernstein, an author, investment adviser, and practicing neurologist.

If you are a market junkie, you may want to keep tabs on the stock market's valuation and how it compares to bonds. For that, go to Thomson Financial/First Call (www.firstcall.com), click through to the market commentary section, and read Part 2 of the analysis.

There, you will find a weekly report that compares the 10-year Treasury note's yield to the price-to-forecasted earnings for the Standard & Poor's 500-stock index. There is a lot of debate over the predictive value of the so-called Fed model. Still, if you check the site regularly, you will be able to hold forth on the stock market's theoretical value, thus greatly impressing the water-cooler crowd.

And how about a little self-promotion? You can find both my Sunday and Wednesday columns at wsj.com, *The Wall Street Journal*'s subscription Web site. My Sunday columns are also available free at sunday.wsj.com. Both sites include an archive function, which you can use to find past articles.

INDEX

Jonathan Clements is the award-winning personal-finance columnist for *The Wall Street Journal*. His "Getting Going" column, which started in October 1994, appears every Wednesday in the *Journal* and every Sunday in more than seventy U.S. newspapers.

Born in London, England, Clements is a graduate of Emmanuel College, Cambridge University. He worked for *Euromoney* magazine in London before moving to the New York area in 1986. Prior to joining the *Journal* in January 1990, he covered mutual funds for *Forbes* magazine.

Clements is also the author of *25 Myths You've Got to Avoid—If You Want to Manage Your Money Right,* published by Simon & Schuster in 1998, and *Funding Your Future: The Only Guide to Mutual Funds You'll Ever Need,* published by Warner Books in 1993.